THE CALM AMIDST THE CHAOS

A Journey Towards Mindfulness and Meditation for the Agitated Soul

---

Gerard Francis

The Calm Amidst the Chaos: A Journey Towards Mindfulness and
Meditation for the Agitated Soul

© 2025 Gerard Francis

First Edition

Published by Paradiddle Publishing
Adelaide, South Australia
www.paradiddle.com.au

ISBN: 978-1-7638638-1-1

All rights reserved. No part of this book may be reproduced, stored in a retrieval system, or transmitted in any form or by any means, electronic, mechanical, photocopying, recording, or otherwise, without the prior written permission of the publisher, except in the case of brief quotations embodied in critical articles or reviews.

This is a work of non-fiction. Some names and identifying details may have been changed to protect the privacy of individuals. Any resemblance to actual persons, living or dead,
is entirely coincidental and unintentional.

Printed in Australia

this book is dedicated to my soulmate Neeru,
the one who loves me
cares for me
believes in me
respects and honours me

more than I do myself

you're my home
you are the calm amidst my chaos

I will love you forever

Table Of Contents

The Pearls Amidst the Paradoxes Intro. — 11

Prelude to the Calm & Chaos Paradox — 12
The Pearls Amidst the Paradoxes™ — 13
Paradox Meets Pearl — 13
Chaos Meets Calm — 14
The Outrage Gauge™ — 15
Tone and Style — 15
Final Introductory Thoughts — 16

1 I'm an Agitated Soul — 17

Warning: Stormfront Approaching — 17
Drowning in the Mud — 19
Washing Away the Mud — 20
Teacher or Tyrant? — 21
Reciprocity is Not a Pity Party — 22
Unexpected Pearls — 24
A Time for Change — 25
There's Salvation in the Calm — 26

2 The Foundations of Mindfulness — 29

Ancient Wisdom, Modern Relevance — 31
Please Don't Judge Me — 32
The Paradox and the Toothbrush — 34
I Can't Find the Off Switch! — 36

3 Mindfulness in Action — 39

The Coffee Conundrum — 39

Sweet Taste of Transformation — 40
A Sensory Smorgasbord — 41
Bittersweet Scent of Yesterday — 43
The Dance & Detox Combo — 44
The Dynamic Duo of Doom — 45
Little Cathartic Acts of Anarchy — 46

4 Where Did Agitation Begin? — 47

The First Encounter — 49
Early Life: Loved but Lost — 49
The Paradox and the Potato Chip — 51
Paragons of P — 52
The Fallout — 53
From the Melting Pot into the Cauldron — 54
The Lure of Something Greater — 56
That Which Lurks in the Shadows — 57
Post-Mortem Brutality — 59
The Soon-to-be-Old You — 60

5 The Transformation Begins — 63

Separation and the Clarity it Provides — 64
Ego is not a Dirty Word — 65
The Paradox and the Ego — 67
Fear Nothing, Expect Nothing — 69

6 Mindfulness... Meet the Edge of Mayhem — 71

Who *is* That Behind the Curtain? — 72
Come Out, Come Out, Wherever You Are — 74
Emotional Bias: Naked and Afraid — 75
Fess Up, Who Did That? — 77
Just Keep on Punching — 77
Combatants ... To Your Corners — 78

7 The Mindfulness vs Meditation Debate   87

Mindfulness: Brewed to Order   89
Two Tools, One You   91
Full Awareness: Your New Superpower   92
Inner Peace, But at What Cost?   94
Cracking the Chicken and the Egg Paradox   95
Where To Begin: Wherever You Can   96
Momentum Matters   97
The Awkward Truth   97
More Authentic Inking, Less Self Thinking   98
Not Quite What You Were Expecting, Right   99
Just Get Started   100

8 Embracing Mindfulness and Meditation   103

How Deep is the Pocket?   104
Too Small for Thought, Too Big for Words   106
Finding Meditation in Most Unexpected Places   107
From Flow to Focus: The Mindfulness Shift   108
Mindfulness in Motion   109
Are You Living, or Merely Existing?   109
The Stars of the Show   112
Where are the Stars of the Musical?   113
No Rules, Just Reconnection   114

9 Practising Mindfulness and Meditation   115

Perfect Practise Makes Perfect Meditation   116
Mindfulness Over Matter   122
Open the Door to Present Moment Awareness   128

10 Breaking Out of the Habit Trap   129

Habits: The Rhythm's Beneath Action   132
The Neocortex: The Role of Your Inner Strategist   136

Stop the Ride. I Want to Get Off!   142
Tools for Habit Change   145

11   The Science of Sticky   149

Mindfulness Tools for Habit Change   150
Get Sticky With It   152
Cattle Prod or Carrot Cake?   153
Life Through the Lens of Sticky Mindfulness   155
From Agitation to Architect   157

12   Navigating Life's Curveballs   159

Curveball: To Be or Not to Be   161
Break in the Clouds … or the Eye in the Storm   163
Triviality: Get in the Back Seat – And Stay There   166
Sting Like a Bee   167
Has the Buck Stopped Yet?   168
INVICTUS by William Ernest Henley   170
The Straw That Unbroke the Camel's Back   171

13   Overcoming Your Biggest Obstacle   173

When the Ashes Settle…   186

14   Finding Your Inner Calm   189

Are You a Teddy Bear or a Grizzly Bear?   191
Don't Shoot the Messenger   192
Peace-ing it all Together   193
Only Two Things in Life are True …   200

15   The Agitation Autopsy   203

The Hardest Thing to do is the Easiest Thing to Start   213
Flip the Switch … Really   215

Before You Holster the Toolkit   217
I Think I'll Sleep Well Tonight...   219

16 Your Journey Forward   **221**

Intent Without Action is Just Drift   222
Let Your Resilience Shine Bright   223

17 Embracing Your Transcendent Soul   **225**

The Proof is in the Pudding   227
Well...What are you Waiting For?   228

The Calm Companion Field Guide   **231**

- 👀 Visual Index   233
- 📖 Agitation Autopsy Roadmap   236
- ⚓ Inspirational Anchors   237
- 🧘 Mindfulness & Meditation Practices   239
- 🎯 Habit Transformation Tools   239
- 🧩 Emotional Resilience Strategies   240
- 🌱 Self-Compassion & Self-Care   240
- ⚔ Mindfulness in Battle   241
- ◯ Foundational Insights   241
- 📕 Starting the Journey   242
- 👤 Continuing the Journey   242
- 🧠 Inner Mapping Tools   243
- 🧰 Emergency Calm Kit   244
- 🔍 The Mirror Questions   244
- 🐝 The Sting in the Tale (Reprise)   245

The Sting in the Tale   **247**

Introduction

The Pearls Amidst the Paradoxes

"The eternal paradox of human life is that we are always striving for something that, when attained, reveals its shortcomings." – Simone Weil

Before we dive right in, I want to be upfront with you. I'm not a therapist. I'm not a psychologist, psychiatrist, counsellor, or social worker. I'm not a sage either. Nor am I a guru, shaman, healer, or spiritual teacher.

I'm just like you: an ordinary person, navigating life's chaos, craving clarity, and searching for the centre of my own universe; the place where the agitation ends and the healing begins.

I may be only one step further down the road than you. Who knows? But like you, I've lived the chaos, and I have wrestled with it. I just wrote down what I learned along the way. And if my musings help even a single person sidestep just one plunge pool disguised as a pothole, then it will have been worth it.

This world has never made sense to me. That might sound like an odd statement, but it's true. I've always felt a peculiar form of disconnection from it. Moreover, the more I tried to make sense of it all, the more difficult it became.

In the process, the frustration that accumulated in me over time manifested as agitation that, in the end, became too heavy to lift. That's the reason I embarked on a pilgrimage to transcend my agitated soul.

If these pages hold any wisdom at all, it's because the truths inside are born from experience, not expertise. So don't expect this book, or the series it's a part of, to contain ethereal wisdom written on a mountaintop.

This book was forged in the trenches, at eye level, with bruises and beatings *served on the side*. But it started with the same doubts and hopes you might carry right now.

Prelude to the Calm & Chaos Paradox

And therein lies the reason this series exists. It is a lived exploration from within which opened my eyes to the world of paradoxes. And what better place to begin the series than the journey to finding calm amidst my chaos?

When I stumbled into the world of paradoxes, they quickly pulled me in. I felt like I was being sucked into an overwhelming whirlpool of instant clarity.

What followed became a crusade for me. The more I was drawn in by them, the more I questioned, challenged, scrapped and researched until eventually ... I decided to write about them.

What I've discovered is this: *the most powerful insights, the kind that genuinely change us, often rise from the tension between opposing forces.*

And that tension is right where this series lives.

My agitation is not the poetic kind; far from it. It's a relentless grind of anxiety, anger, impulse, and emotional combustion. The kind that wears down your edges until even stillness feels like friction.

If you've felt even a flicker of that same storm, then I'm thrilled that you are reading this book. I can only pray now that it helps you find a quieter corner of your own mind, because that's all it's really trying to do.

The Pearls Amidst the Paradoxes™

Welcome to a journey unlike most self-help offerings: a series of *self-reflection* pieces built on experience, reflection, and framed by contradiction.

Each book in *The Pearls Amidst the Paradoxes*™ series seeks to uncover pearls of wisdom born of friction. Genuine insights unearthed from real-world disorder fused into the paradoxes of life.

This series explores the space between clarity and confusion, surrender and control, peace and pressure.

Life isn't simple and wisdom isn't spoon-fed. It's built in paradox. And if you're willing to walk through that discomfort, I'm living proof that there are pearls to be found.

Paradox Meets Pearl

A pearl is a symbol of wisdom and beauty formed through adversity. It begins as an irritant lodged inside an oyster, gradually layered with nacre until it becomes something precious and beautiful.

That process isn't smooth. It's slow. It's painful. But the result is a timeless beauty, born of tension.

Paradoxes, like pearls, begin with friction. On the surface, they seem absurd or self-contradictory. But when you sit with them—

really sit—they reveal themselves. A paradox challenges your assumptions and demands you look again.

This series treats personal struggle the same way. The irritants in your life can produce pearls if you're willing to engage them, hidden treasures buried inside adversity.

Look at it this way. Paradoxes aren't riddles to solve; they're truths to unlock. Each contradiction you face holds insight just beneath its tension.

The series challenges you to look beneath tension instead of skating on it, to discover those insights. It encourages you to lean into your discomfort and develop a deeper understanding of why it exists.

Most importantly, it aims to nurture a belief in you that the more uncomfortable it feels, the more transformation it likely offers.

As Søren Kierkegaard aptly stated,

> *"The paradox is really the pathos of intellectual life, and just as only great souls are exposed to passions, so only great thinkers are exposed to what I call paradoxes, which are nothing else than grandiose thoughts in embryo."*

That's what's at the heart of this series: illuminating those unborn truths that hide inside your life's contradictions.

Chaos Meets Calm

Calm Amidst the Chaos: A Journey Towards Mindfulness and Meditation for the Agitated Soul kicks off this series.

It does not need to be read alongside any other book in this series. It stands alone in its pursuit to tame life's madness.

It invites you to wrestle with the tension that exists between your chaos and your yearning for calm.

Sometimes that's what it takes to make sense of your inner friction. This book encourages you to harvest personal wisdom from the spaces most people avoid.

It's not always tidy, but it's honest. And honesty is where transformation starts.

The Outrage Gauge™

Before we go any further, I should explain the gauge on the front cover.

I call it the *Outrage Gauge*™ and it's a handy little visual cue to prepare you for my emotional intensity in each book of the series.

It's designed to spare your system the shock of unexpected paradoxical rage. While some paradoxes simply invite gentle contemplation, others ignite a fierce passion in me that I can't help but release. It's part of my therapy.

As the dial on the front cover indicates, *Calm Amidst the Chaos* sits firmly in the former category. It's a slow simmer; more soul-searching than soapboxing, so you're safe … for now.

Fear not, however. If it's heat you're after, other books in the series contain paradoxes so fiery they spark a full-blown emotional inferno in me. I'm confident they'll do the trick.

So, consider this book your gentle entry point, and your early warning for what lies ahead.

Tone and Style

You may also notice, the words don't sit quietly on the page. They carry a certain lilt, a rhythm, and sometimes a raised eyebrow. That's entirely deliberate.

The tone and style are as much a part of the message as the ideas themselves, shaping how they land in your head and your heart.

The series is written with honesty, warmth, and the occasional passionate digression. You'll find philosophy, a few rants, and more than a generous sprinkle of well-intentioned punchlines.

Not to mention a rattling of your cage every now and then, encouraging you to look deeper into yourself for a greater overall experience and outcome.

Most importantly, the messages are loud and clear. They offer practical wisdom and insights that are easy to grasp and apply.

Final Introductory Thoughts

The Calm Amidst the Chaos: A Journey Towards Mindfulness and Meditation for the Agitated Soul invites you to slow down, tune in, and gently interrogate your chaos with compassion.

And while it's part of a broader conversation, *Calm Amidst the Chaos* stands alone as a quiet rebellion against a world that won't stop shouting.

If you are suffering from chaos overload, this book is all you need. My hope is to empower you to *embrace change*, navigate challenges with greater ease, and achieve a more balanced, fulfilling life.

At least, that is the aim, but you must be both willing and able. Change doesn't happen passively.

You're not a caterpillar, destined to become a butterfly.

You're a person with real hopes and dreams, but your dreams of flight mean little if you refuse to leave the ground.

My parting words to you are these: take time to reflect, listen inwardly, and act on the insights you uncover that truly resonate with you.

Let's embark on this journey together. Embrace the paradox, uncover the pearls, and let your transformation commence.

Here's to a stronger, more resilient, and deeply fulfilled you.

1

I'm an Agitated Soul

I am an *Agitated Soul!* There, I've said it! I have been unofficially saddled with the self-proclaimed title: *world's foremost authority on enduring it.* A restless spirit bludgeoning my way through the chaotic undercurrents of my own existence.

Warning: Stormfront Approaching

This agitation has been my constant companion, an unwelcome shadow clinging to my very essence like a leech, sucking the tranquillity from me.

But why? Who in their right mind would choose to live with an *agitated soul?* Is it even a choice? That's the million-dollar question, right?

Perhaps it's genetic or the weight of social expectations. Maybe it's parental conditioning or plain, dumb luck. Or could it be the product of a lifetime spent indulging in questionable and dishonourable pursuits?

Whatever the cause, this unrest has eaten away at me my whole life, like rust on piano strings.

Don't get me wrong, I currently live a beautiful life that I share with a beautiful soul, but it did not come cheap. It was forged from battle; some I created, some I stumbled into, others I had thrust upon me. A few were even conjured from thin air.

And it was this realisation, a quiet reckoning, that allowed the seed of change to finally germinate.

Navigating life while highly agitated, often feels like I'm holding a handful of sparks in a paper bag. Inside, everything flares violently while on the outside, I pretend not to burn.

Sometimes the anguish erupts with such force that it manifests physically, making it feel like my soul is being peeled, one layer at a time.

Even simple, dare I say harmless, moments would spiral into chaos. I recall more than one occasion being so overcome by my agitation, I had no idea what set me off—not before, not during, not after.

In the heat of battle, all I knew was that I was consumed. How does that happen? How does a trigger fierce enough to ignite me disappear from existence? How could I have no recollection of the firestarter?

Still, I'm proud to say these firestorms now flicker more than they rage. A quiet testament to resilience and growth, perhaps.

And it's that resilience, through hard-won skirmishes, that I want to share. Because, although far from conquered, it's that grit that broke the back of my torment.

If you too carry the weight of an *agitated soul*, I suspect you've felt this torment firsthand.

It's not pleasant to endure, is it? After decades dealing with this emotional self-sabotage, eventually something must give.

That's why I'm writing this book and baring my soul (pun absolutely intended). To exorcise my demons, yes. But just as importantly, to assist you with your escape from the oppression agitation wields.

Thankfully, I've learned to read these emotional currents, and I've begun to ride them rather than wrestle against them. With time, I've gained greater control over my reactions and, more importantly, my responses to what triggers them.

Embracing this process has become both a source of strength and a strange kind of adventure toward deeper self-awareness and greater calm.

Drowning in the Mud

Let me be clear, this isn't a deep dive into the murky swamp of my emotional baggage (though, as you've probably already picked up on, there's plenty to wade through).

No, I don't pace the halls or curl up under my desk in a foetal position dribbling, well, not usually anyway. But I do still run afoul of my own misgivings from time to time, and I'm willing to bet you do too.

And that's precisely my point; this is about you. Think of this book as a wide-angle view of what it means to live as an *agitated soul* and how to rise from it.

Use my experiences as a sounding board, a mirror, sometimes even a gentle provocation to peer beneath your emotional bonnet in pursuit of a deeper connection to your *authentic self*.

You'll see that phrase—*authentic self*—surface often in these pages. Because somewhere beneath all that agitation, buried beneath noise, reflex, and tangled emotion, there's a more genuine version of you just waiting to be set free.

While I'm on the topic, when I refer to *Agitated Soul* or *Authentic Self*, I'm not talking about multiple personalities. I'm talking about archetypes. It's my way of naming the forces inside us so we can see them more clearly.

Back to my point, for your *Authentic Self* to be set free, something must shift. Change, I know, is daunting, but it is oh-so-necessary.

Some change will be subtle, like a breeze nudging the tide. But others could hit hard, and you'll need to brace for the discomfort.

Transformation doesn't come from comfort; it comes from the kind of change that shakes you and demands that you grow. I'm sorry to be blunt, but there is no subtle way to frame it.

A word of solace before we do press on, however: if your emotional load becomes too heavy to carry alone, please seek professional support.

The path to self-discovery should be walked with care and never without backup.

It's highly likely you will be revisiting some painful memories along the way, and that is never easy to deal with. You're not expected to do it solo. So, lean on your support network when you need to.

And think of me as your enthusiastic curator, cheering you on, helping you pack wisdom, resilience, and grit with you for the journey ahead.

Washing Away the Mud

Every road that leads to real change begins with action. So, here's the washup: I'd had enough of wallowing in self-pity. Tired of being a prisoner to my own discontent, I finally acted.

I chose to write this book. I had been teetering on the edge of unhealthy self-indulgence, and hellbent on leaping. But now I was done playing the misunderstood star in a one-man pantomime, reciting a soliloquy no one would hear.

And you must be done with it too. Why else would you have picked up this book? There's so much within your grasp, within your control, that can transform you from the inside out.

It's time to stop wallowing in the mud and carve a new path through it. Is it an easy fix? Hell, no! But it is fixable, and at a good pace, if you face it head-on.

Teacher or Tyrant?

Why don't we start simple? How difficult is it to be more kind to yourself? Really. Before you mutter *"easier said than done, mate"* with a double dose of salt, remember, I've been there.

I've lived it and I've got the scars to prove it.

Sometimes a little self-empathy is all it takes. Just stop being so damn hard on yourself. Show a little compassion for the many sordid battles you've already survived.

Those battle scars are your armour; they're not a weakness and not your enemy. Don't fear them, be liberated by them. That's the power self-empathy brings to this fight.

You'll also need courage, and not just a sprinkle. Let's be real, facing life's challenges can often feel like dancing the tango in roller skates on sand … blindfolded.

But here's the grace in it: you don't need all your courage up front. You only need enough to take that first wobbly step into the shadows.

It's like jumping into a pool carved from winter's spine. Your teeth chatter, and you do that awkward little dance at first, but before you know it, you're doing cannonballs.

Then, as you edge deeper into the hurricane of your agitation and push toward the eye of your storm, courage begins to rise, and your transformation takes root. In that moment you'll feel a shift. The storm stops owning you and you start owning the storm.

As you navigate the dark shadows of your fears and uncertainties, you begin to uncover a hidden strength; one that's been waiting for this exact moment to emerge. How powerful is that?

It may feel messy at times, even overwhelming, but every challenge faced becomes a stepping stone toward deeper self-awareness and real self-empowerment.

And, in that space of raw confrontation, not only will you gain deeper insight into your own emotions, but you'll also begin to inspire those around you to face theirs.

That's what I'm hoping to spark with this book.

C'mon! You've got this!

Reciprocity is Not a Pity Party

Let me be honest, the term agitation barely scratches the surface of the volcanic turmoil that's lived in me over the years.

But in the spirit of **kindness**, and for the consideration of those who may not carry the same emotional weight, let's settle on it. Let's call it agitation. A word that carries urgency without overwhelming those who might be so inclined.

It helps us connect while acknowledging the varying degrees of simmering intensity that bubbles beneath the surface in each of us.

Whatever name you give it, you'll need kindness to tame it. Not just the self-kindness we touched on earlier, but the kind you accept from others.

It's not born from pity, however; it's forged through reciprocity. That means you have a responsibility to earn that compassion, to honour it, and meet the givers of it halfway.

I learnt that the hard way. This book and any healing I've found wouldn't exist without mutual grace. I had to do more than accept my beloved's unconditional love. I had to meet it. Match it. Earn it.

And to do that meant offering her something that's never been easy for me: sharing my pain.

No one can help if you don't share what you feel. The love and support I now cherish would've stayed locked away if I hadn't opened up to her.

That's the kind of earned compassion I'm talking about. The commitment to invite someone into your storm and show them your bruises.

When it comes to an *agitated soul* however, I'm afraid that's only half the deal. I know it sounds like I'm asking a lot of you, but that's the cost of undoing years of doing.

The other price you're going to have to pay is, you must learn to temper the outbursts. And the sooner you do, the better for all concerned.

Because if you don't, your loved ones end up shouldering the full weight of your chaos while still trying to offer grace. And that's not a fair trade.

You know what it's like, right? When agitation takes a chokehold, and all you want to do is rant. You're pissed, and you don't have the time, or the inclination to care about the effect your rage has on others.

And that—*right there*—is where the real destruction lives.

Acknowledging your struggles and seeking support can transform agitation into productive dialogue. However, those who love you cannot carry you indefinitely, nor can they decipher your silent rage as if it were a coded cry for help.

Yes, accept their undying love and support, but don't take it for granted. Your loved ones will buckle under the added weight if you do.

That's why this book walks beside you. You've got to step up and prepare for the reciprocity that is required. Kindness is not unrequited. You must develop trust. Trust is everything.

When I finally opened up, everything started falling into place. But it wasn't until I cracked open my chest and poured my chaos onto these pages, that healing truly began.

Splinters of calm amidst my chaos began to appear. Tiny fragments of purpose in the agitation, glinting like crystal shards in the mud.

Now my once tumultuous thoughts are woven into anecdotes and stories. I hope they will resonate with you and others who have weathered similar storms.

But none of this would've been possible without vulnerability. That's the truth. That's my testament.

That's our shared humanity.

Unexpected Pearls

Delving deep into your psyche often reveals unexpected layers of complexity. But that's the mark of true courage, and it's how you unearth the pearls.

Like finding a rogue twenty-dollar note in your jeans pocket; it's surprising, satisfying, and proof that something valuable was there all along.

Resolution begins with understanding. It means unpacking those complexities to see how far they reach.

When you think about it, complex emotions are not too dissimilar from complex equations. There's always an answer.

You just have to take the time to understand the problem first. And when you do, the answer often reveals itself with surprising simplicity.

Like a pearl hidden in the paradoxical grit.

Remember that rush when you finally cracked the algebra question on the end-of-year exam? Surely you want more of that, right?

Every challenge we face has a multitude of possible outcomes, and the answer can take many forms, all shaped by emotion. (More on that soon.)

Think back to a time life threw you off course: a job loss, a betrayal, or the end of a meaningful relationship. How did you respond?

Did your demons take the wheel without your permission?

Now imagine that same moment through a calm lens. Difficult to do, I know, but they're worlds apart, aren't they?

That's *why* we are *agitated souls*. Calm is difficult for us. It never comes easy.

And it happens to the best of us, so please, find solace in knowing you're not alone; I, for one, am with you.

Finding yourself trapped in that whirlwind of emotion, where every small trigger decouples you from sanity is an unpleasant experience. I've lived it and it's no picnic.

That's why you and I are now walking this road side by side, after all.

Navigating the intricacies of human emotion isn't about treating symptoms; it's about creating space for healing and understanding, so calm can twinkle amidst the chaos.

A Time for Change

In the pandemonium of modern life with no instruction booklet, where curveballs are the constant and inner peace feels like fiction, we all need a light to guide us. Sometimes that light is faint, but even a flicker can keep you moving forward, away from the dark.

I wrote this book to be a lighthouse in my own darkness. Now, I hope it shines for you too, as you forge ahead toward the intimidating centre of you.

I pray these words offer you more than anecdotes. They're written to support you with powerful practices of mindfulness and meditation, and deliver emotional clarity wrapped in love, empathy, and compassion.

I want to reiterate one more time, I am not a therapist. I'm not a psychologist, psychiatrist, counsellor, social worker, or any other professional with the word therapist at the end of their title.

Nor am I a sage, a guru, shaman, spiritual teacher, guide, or healer of any kind. I'm just searching for that place where the agitation ends, and the healing begins.

All I can offer you is empathy and some cold, hard truth about the journey into the eye of my storm.

And here's a small taste of that cold, hard truth: the storm wasn't all mine, it never was. Most of it belonged to others.

I simply and naively latched onto the lot of it; an unconscious accumulation of all the *shit* I was told I might need one day.

I suspect you're nodding in violent agreement right now.

But here's the thing. A day came when I realised the weight of it was too heavy for me to withstand. There's a reason it's called emotional baggage.

There's Salvation in the Calm

So, my friend, if you're tired of being tossed about by the unpredictable tides of your own existence, if you long to reclaim calm and inner harmony, then I'm damn glad I'm in this with you.

Let's take this ride together.

Let's board this journey towards a calmer, more grounded you, where inner peace isn't a far-off promise, but something you get to claim and keep.

A life where the ups and downs of the universe no longer dictate your emotional state, and calm becomes your steadfast companion.

So, what can you expect as you navigate the murky waters of your own agitation? Honestly, that depends on how you choose to meet the process.

I know that might sound cliché or like a throwaway line, but it's the honest truth. No one can impart anything if you don't have the mindset to receive it.

What I can promise, though, is this: you'll be met with honesty. And let's be real; sometimes the truth is tough to swallow.

It's like biting into a sour lemon, when you're expecting something sweet. It's sour at first, then sharp enough to wake something up.

So brace yourself. The journey won't always be smooth, but if you stick with it, if you meet honesty halfway, it might just carve out your path forward.

And in that truth, may you find salvation in the calm ... amidst your chaos.

The Calm Amidst the Chaos

2

The Foundations of Mindfulness

If you're anything like me, your mind is often a raging storm, and your thoughts are arguing like pundits on a panel show, debating emotional truths they're wildly unqualified to handle.

Then, while dealing with that hostile frame of mind, someone cuts you off in traffic, and the *experts* suggest you meditate? Sure, okay.

If it were that easy, everyone would be enlightened and floating three inches off the ground. But instead, we're here, still agitated, restless, and occasionally we find ourselves yelling at slow walkers under our breath.

That's the plight of an *agitated soul*. This world demands calm but serves up chaos like an all-you-can-eat buffet that we gorge on until our soul loses its flavour.

So, how do we tackle that? How do we break that cycle in times of desperate need? Simple: we take the chaos, carve out some calm, and make peace with both. Never forget, the calm is *amidst* the chaos, it always will be.

Unfortunately, that's the world we live in. It's why we are the way we are. But by drawing a line between the two (which will take practice), we give ourselves a clear space we can gravitate towards when we need to escape the agitation.

> Take the chaos, carve out some calm, and make peace with both.

Before we delve deeper into the practical stuff, let's pause and reflect on the rich history that underpins each practice. This is our moment to ground ourselves in where it all began.

Misunderstandings are rife in our culture and many stem from a lack of knowledge at the most fundamental level. So, let's *honour the roots* before turning to the how-to.

Defining mindfulness and its benefits for mental well-being is far more layered than it first appears. While the practice of mindfulness has historical roots spanning centuries, the 20th century turned it into *training* for mental health.

This shift in perspective led to an explosion of interest in mindfulness, which by the turn of the century had become a tired and worn-out buzzword.

Unfortunately, this commercialisation has often diluted its essence, reducing a profound spiritual practice to mere stress-relief techniques and trendy wellness fads.

True mindfulness encompasses much more than just relaxation; it involves cultivating present-moment awareness and non-judgmental acceptance. This can significantly improve emotional resilience and overall mental clarity.

Recognising its deeper meaning beyond the superficial applications helps reclaim its original purpose.

Ancient Wisdom, Modern Relevance

The history of mindfulness dates back to ancient spiritual traditions, particularly within Buddhism. It was practised as a form of meditation designed to cultivate awareness and presence in the moment.

This practice extends back over 2,500 years, when Siddhartha Gautama, known as the Buddha, advocated mindfulness as a path to both enlightenment and liberation from suffering.

Over the centuries that ensued, mindfulness has been woven into various religious and philosophical systems across Asia. It evolved through practices such as Zen meditation in Japan and Vipassana in Southeast Asia, each offering its own doorway to stillness.

In recent decades, this ancient practice has gained traction in Western cultures. Figures like Jon Kabat-Zinn, who adapted mindfulness for Western medical settings, were at the forefront of this movement west.

The growing body of scientific research supporting its mental health benefits, such as reducing stress and anxiety, has further propelled its popularity beyond spiritual circles into everyday life.

Understanding the rich and intricate history of mindfulness not only highlights its profound roots, steeped in ancient traditions and practices, but also reveals just how needed it is in our frantic, fast-paced modern world.

Today, stress and distractions are ubiquitous, and mindfulness emerges as a powerful antidote to combat this constant barrage. It has never been more needed than it is right now.

The historical foundations illuminate how mindfulness helps cultivate awareness of thoughts, emotions, and surroundings.

The complexities of daily life, whether it's the pressures of work deadlines or the constant barrage of digital noise, are unrelenting.

True mindfulness offers a sanctuary for reflection and tranquillity. It's a weapon against distractions, a way to reclaim ourselves before the world pulls us apart.

Please Don't Judge Me

We all walk, talk, think, and make thousands of choices every day. But here's the real question: how many of these actions are performed with mindfulness?

More importantly, do our daily interactions stem from a place of conscious awareness and intentionality? To explore this properly, let's look more closely at what mindfulness really means here.

Mindfulness refers to the practice of being fully present in the moment, acknowledging our thoughts, feelings, and surroundings *without judgement*. That's an important distinction.

It encompasses an acute awareness that allows us to engage thoughtfully with our environment rather than simply reacting impulsively or habitually. It's the difference between living with intention and merely reacting to life.

An *agitated soul*, however, is often blinded by overwhelm. Are you like me, catching your inner voice muttering with alarming regularity, *"I don't care that the problem is fixed! I'm bloody agitated."* Does this sound familiar? Crazy, right?

Our sense of agitation can be so devastatingly relentless, it becomes what we identify with, and we dismiss the present moment like it owes us back rent. What an absurd existence.

By exploring *true* mindfulness, we can better assess whether our behaviours reflect a deliberate choice grounded in awareness, or if they're merely automatic responses influenced by internal and external pressures.

Furthermore, understanding this distinction can lead us toward more meaningful choices that align with our true values and aspirations.

By incorporating mindfulness techniques into our routines, such as meditation (which we will explore in more detail soon), focussed breathing exercises, or mindful walking, we can reclaim moments of calm amidst this modern chaos.

Ultimately, embracing this age-old practice enriches us. It equips us with essential tools to face life's challenges and produces clarity sharp enough to *cut through the mental fog*.

So, how does this relate to you? What aspects of mindfulness do you need to harness? That's precisely what you're about to find out in these pages.

As we have already covered, mindfulness deserves to be more than a trendy buzzword or a *passing phase*; it's a powerful practice that has stood the test of time that can significantly enhance your daily life by treating your agitated state.

Additionally, mindfulness produces practical intrinsic benefits too. It can improve focus, reduce other forms of stress, and sharpen decision-making.

Consider what being present in the moment can do for you. Whether during a challenging task or simply engaging with loved ones, it can help you develop deeper connections and more meaningful experiences, with much less agitation to boot. Who doesn't want that?

Therefore, by harnessing mindfulness techniques you tap into your inner resilience, enabling you to navigate challenges with the grace of someone who's agreed to make peace with chaos.

Mindfulness may sound simple enough, but like all good things, it takes time to establish. In a world so conditioned to instant gratification, I fear very few of our future generations will have the patience to cultivate and preserve this ancient lost art.

There's no way to sugarcoat this, change is difficult—plain and simple. We'll be returning to this truth time and time again because it's that important.

And here's another hard truth: if you want to improve anything in life, *something* must change.

So, if after you begin practising, it starts feeling overwhelming, then ease into something more your pace. There's no timer running here and this is definitely not a sprint. Just slow things down a little but *do not leave the track!*

Perhaps simply practising gratitude for a few days will be enough to continue the momentum. Being *mindful* enough to say thank you more often, or even just practising observing your thoughts *without judgement*.

This will help consolidate your foundation for more deeply rooted mindfulness practices in time.

The Paradox and the Toothbrush

Here's a practical case in point. How many times have you brushed your teeth while staring straight through the reflection of your own eyes peering menacingly back at you, completely unaware of the moment, lost in distraction?

This experience is far too common in our frenetic existence. Routine actions become automatic behaviours, disconnected from awareness and sacrificed to keep pace.

But you brushed your teeth, right? So, how did you manage to achieve that without thinking about it? Without *experiencing* it?

When you break it down, brushing your teeth is a complex motor neural activity. If you don't believe me, try it with your *non-dominant hand* and see if you can do it without stabbing yourself in the gums.

That's where habit forming comes into the picture. We'll explore this deeper when the time's right. Still, it's worth planting a seed about the role habits play now because, well, let's face it, you'll be a lot easier on yourself when you realise that your *agitated soul* is not entirely of your own doing. Neuroscience plays a big part.

Here's what it looks like. While your conscious mind was busy ruminating over that meeting that went off the rails yesterday, your subconscious was quietly managing the task of brushing your teeth.

It's pretty wild to think about how powerful this process is. You may have completely zoned out, yet your subconscious was deftly orchestrating every move with precision.

Rinse and repeat enough and voilà! A new automated routine without you even realising it. With the assistance of time and repetition, you have transformed a mundane activity into a well-oiled habit.

But that comes at a cost; your enjoyment of the moment, of any moment, is sacrificed when it becomes automated by the subconscious mind.

What does that all mean?

Your ruminating has *robbed you of a small piece of life*.

And here's the kicker: during the habit creation cycle, a mutual agreement is struck between the conscious and subconscious minds. At some point, the responsibility of managing a habit is handed over by the conscious mind to the subconscious.

But your conscious mind hands that responsibility over with an attitude. Those habits have been shaped by your personality, and if your personality profile is *agitated*, then guess what...

Isn't it fascinating (and frightening) how our daily routines can reflect our inner chaos, showing just how intertwined our minds and actions really are!

And this is where it gets really scary.

Now swap brushing your teeth for a scene with your agitation in full flight. See—scary, right?

I Can't Find the Off Switch!

That's your subconscious running agitation-laced patterns because that's what it's been fed for so many years.

Have you ever been so agitated that you can't switch it off? You've acknowledged your agitation, and you want it to cease. But, goddammit, you're going to be agitated whether others like it or not.

Are you ready for the truth?

Your agitation is constantly simmering beneath the surface in your subconscious mind. *You* only find out about it when it's too late, when it floods back into your conscious mind. What?

Let me explain. Think of your subconscious as a loving parent and your agitation as a naughty child.

The loving parent (subconscious) can only take so much. Eventually they're going to say to the other parent (conscious) *"I can't deal with him anymore! You take care of it"*.

Now it really is *your* problem because it's now conscious.

In other words, subconscious routines or *habits* are not part of the conscious mind's daily workings. They're nestled deep in the cavernous void of your subconscious mind. They run silently in

**Neither the past nor the future is in our control.
Not one ounce of either!**

the background until some part of it is forced into conscious thought.

The subconscious swallows and manages all the data your conscious mind (aka the *neocortex*) can't handle. But as illustrated above, it's a two-way street.

Now relate that back to everyday life. It's alarming to realise how often we miss the simple act of being present because we *choose* to focus on other things. And in many circumstances, things that feed our agitation.

Our thoughts, shaped by our disposition, drift into a haze filled with worries about the day ahead, or regrets from the past.

It becomes cyclic: *habitual*. Before long, ruminating about what was, or worrying about what is yet to be, has become *normal life*.

What we *should* be doing is stopping to smell the roses once in a while—literally. Granting our mind escape from *this moment* to feast on the chaos is a disease, and utterly futile.

It's as if we're all suffering from a mild epidemic of distraction! Did I say *mild*? Yeah, that was generous. What a huge waste of mental energy.

Think about it; neither of those *moments in time* (past or future) is in your control! Not one ounce of either. So why do we give them so much airtime? Ridiculous!

By pausing, even during mundane tasks, we can begin to cultivate mindfulness that enhances our daily experiences.

Embracing this practice can transform ordinary moments into opportunities for self-reflection, leading to a more enriched existence on this merry-go-round we call life.

So, next time you find yourself brushing your teeth in a foggy daze, challenge yourself to anchor your thoughts in the present. It could lead to profound shifts in how you show up in each moment.

The Calm Amidst the Chaos

3

Mindfulness in Action

All right, my friend, let's whet your appetite with some practical gear: three simple mindfulness practices to set you on the right path.

They'll sharpen your awareness and anchor you in real-time, easing you into the tougher work ahead: unravelling the mystery of how you became an agitated soul in the first place.

You might even savour this calm before the storm, knowing the waters won't always be smooth, but the voyage will be worth it in the long run.

The Coffee Conundrum

First up, try the classic *mindful coffee sipping*. It's a simple illustration of what being in a state of mindfulness really means. Here's how it works.

Instead of wolfing down that cup like it's the last complimentary party pie in an overcrowded bar, take a moment to actually taste it. Is it bitter? Sweet? Does it remind you of that time you accidentally drank decaf and questioned your existence?

I will never forget the day the penny dropped for me on this one. In all honesty, this moment might've sparked everything for me. I wish I could say that it was a conscious choice, but alas, I cannot.

I parked my car after arriving at work, then leaned across to the passenger seat and dragged my over-laden backpack across the centre console with a grunt.

As I did, my attention was drawn to the empty takeaway coffee cup in the cup holder. I can't explain why it caught my eye, but I'm glad it did.

In that instant, I had an epiphany. I thought to myself, almost in a trance, *"During the commute, I consumed the whole damn cup of coffee and didn't taste a single drop."*

What a revelation! How is it possible that I engaged all my senses with that cup of coffee, yet none registered in my conscious mind?

I began to think about all the associated interactions: the touch of the cup, the smell of the beans, the bitter taste of the coffee, the feeling of pain when I spilled the boiling beverage on my leg, the gurgling sound as I sipped the coffee through the hole in the lid, and the sound of the pencil piercing the lid to let more air flow (they never make those vent holes big enough).

All those life experiences had passed me by because I wasn't in a state of mindfulness. I was in my default, agitated state. Starting to see the pattern yet?

Sweet Taste of Transformation

That moment genuinely changed my life. I knew then that my *mindless consumeristic behaviour* had to go, and mindfulness must be its successor. If I were going to drink a cup of coffee, I would make sure all sensory perceptions registered in my conscious mind.

I hasten to point out, I didn't know it as *'mindfulness'* back then, but I certainly understood the moment and what it meant.

It meant paying attention to *real life* unfolding on the outside, instead of being trapped in the *melodramatic soap opera* playing out on the inside.

It hit me like a ton of bricks.

I realised that all the mindless consumerism I had been caught up in just wasn't cutting it anymore. From that moment I made a pact with myself; if I was going to eat a burger, I was going to *taste* it. If I was going to listen to music I was going to *hear* it.

And if I was going to sip on an extra hot, large soy latte with half a sugar, you better believe I was going to *savour* every last drop goddangit. I was committed to soaking in all the smells, sounds, and textures life offered!

Simply put, embracing that shift meant enjoying life more fully. Noticing the little joys that had previously slipped through the cracks while being overrun by my inner monologue.

It's amazing how such a simple change can lead to such profound transformations.

A Sensory Smorgasbord

Next up is *the five senses walk*. Take a stroll and consciously notice five things you see (yes, even the neighbour's questionable garden gnome), four things you hear, three things you can touch (preferably not sharp objects), two things you smell (hopefully not anything from yesterday's lunch), and one thing you can taste.

This was another epiphanic moment for me. I never understood walking as a pastime. To me, walking was getting from one place to the next.

Naturally, the modes of transport changed through the years, just like they did for most people; first came pedals, then petrol, until walking quietly packed its bags and left home for good.

Thankfully, I was born with a passion for sports in my blood, so my exercise routine was never starved. It was satiated by the copious number of sports I indulged in.

So, if I was getting my fill of exercise and outdoor lifestyle, why the hell would I walk anywhere? What a drag!

Seriously, though, who has time for it? Walking just seemed like too much time-consuming hard work when there were way more exciting ways to break a sweat.

And don't get me started on running as a pastime; it's just not my thing. Unless I'm chasing after a ball like a *hyperactive Labrador*, you won't catch me running for the sake of running.

My younger brother is obsessed with running marathons, and honestly, all I can do is shake my head in wonder, but hey, to each their own.

But boy, how things can change.

Just a few years ago, if you had told me I'd become a walking enthusiast, I would have chortled in your general direction, offered you a couch cushion for comfort, and suggested you take a nap.

And now, walking is my thing. It's not quite an obsession, but I have a newfound fondness for it. Why, you ask? Because of the five senses walk.

It opened up the present moment to me in ways I never thought possible. Suddenly, I'm not just moving from point A to point B; I'm living life in high definition through the practice.

Give it a try. Really hone in on your sensory receptors. The order doesn't matter; just tune out your mind chatter and tune in to the present moment.

What do you see that you've not noticed before? The unusual colour of a neighbour's front door, the meticulously manicured garden down the street, the classic muscle car in the garage around the corner.

What about the sounds? There is a nature reserve nearby where I live, teeming with birdlife. When I first tried this exercise, I was gobsmacked by their collective volume.

How could I have not noticed it before? It shows you how powerful focus can be, especially when we're focussing on the wrong things—the mental traffic, the ruminations, the regrets.

Bittersweet Scent of Yesterday

Then there's smell. The most powerful sense connected with special memories. The scent of freshly cut grass drifting through the air like nostalgic perfume.

The lingering aroma of the pine needles that litter the walking path, a tantalising waft of authentic home-grown Italian cooking radiating from the kitchen of someone's home as you pass by.

It's interesting to note that smell is neurologically linked to the part of the brain that manages emotion. The other senses are rerouted via a *relay station* in the brain.

That's why the sense of smell can give us such vivid memory recall.

It's why a whiff of sunscreen can teleport you to a beach holiday from 20 years ago, or why the scent of sawdust might summon vivid memories of your grandfather's workshop.

And let's not forget touch and taste. When was the last time you reached out and brushed the leaves of a passing tree?

All these experiences are yours for the taking. They're the very things that make life so rich. So, why are we so prepared to let them slip by, trading them for the self-inflicted torment of worry and regret, or the mindless banality of *social media?*

Is this what *sickness of the soul* looks like in the modern age?

Sure, it can be fun to stay connected online, but at what cost? We're missing out on the joy of feeling the sun on our skin or savouring that first bite of a delicious meal.

It's time to shake off that mental clutter and truly embrace the world around us, because those little experiences make life worth living.

The Dance & Detox Combo

That leads us to our final mindfulness warm-up, *the technology detox dance party*.

Here it is: drop your phone, *kill the doomscroll*, crank the tunes, and move. Even for just fifteen minutes.

It really is that simple. Nothing resets a restless soul quite like letting go.

Remember the old adage, *dance like nobody's watching, sing like nobody's listening?*

I can hear you now: *'What? Are you mad? People will think I'm a git!'*. No, they won't because nobody's watching. Truly, this could be the most powerful thing you embody.

Let me tell you why.

This practice isn't just about shaking off stress; it's a powerful way to reconnect with your authentic self. It provides an opportunity to release pent-up energy, and this really hits home for agitated souls like us.

You'll be in transition for some time, which means, you're going to *relapse* every now and then. And if you don't have a release valve for those times when your relapse is severe, you're flirting with danger.

Your agitated soul doesn't need an invitation to pull you back under. Trust me—this one deserves your full attention.

There's an old saying, *misery likes company*, and it couldn't be more apt when you think about how agitated minds often get stuck in a loop of self-consciousness.

It's like agitation and self-consciousness are handcuffed together, dragging each other down in a never-ending cycle of overthinking and doubt.

The Dynamic Duo of Doom

When you're agitated, do you fall into the trap of comparing your life to *perfect lives* of others? Or worrying more about what people think?

And in the end, all it does is fuel your agitated state even more. I refer to the pairing of agitation and self-consciousness as *the dynamic duo of doom*.

**Self-consciousness pulls us inward and covers us with doubt.
Self-awareness gently guides us outward to experience life.**

Let's take a moment to think about that. There's something remarkable in how self-consciousness and self-awareness are so diametrically opposed.

What might that reveal about who we are and why we're this way?

Self-consciousness fixates on what others *might* be thinking, stirring awkwardness, heightening anxiety, and fanning the flames of our agitation.

At times it drives us into such intense hyper-focus that it paralyses us.

Self-awareness, by contrast, is about understanding our own thoughts, emotions, and motivations, free from the weight of external pressure.

One pulls us inward with doubt, while the other gently guides us outward, helping us see who we are in context with the world.

The contrast is striking, and the shaping of our experiences runs just as deep. Sometimes our choices can mean the difference between being amused by something or being agitated by it.

Which outcome is more appealing? You choose.

Little Cathartic Acts of Anarchy

When you let go of self-consciousness and truly express yourself, whether through dance or any other pursuit, it can be incredibly liberating.

Well, what are you waiting for? Blast your playlist at full volume and let the rebellion begin. You really do have nothing to lose.

And who knows, *little acts of anarchy* might instantly transform your mood and unlock a freedom you never thought possible.

Remember, nobody's watching. Nobody's listening. Don't let *you* be the reason you remain in an agitated state. You are more powerful than you think, so *stand tall and own it*.

Okay, now that we've grounded ourselves with a few warm-up practices, let's dive into the wild ride of how we became the agitated souls we are today.

Let's be honest, our quest for self-awareness is going to take some time. So, by diving into the *why*, at least we'll have a treasure trove of comedic material to keep us entertained along the way.

4

Where Did Agitation Begin?

All right, *Agitated Soul*. It's time to hunt down the roots of your unease like a detective in a crime thriller.

No sugar-coating, no self-pity, just cold, hard truth leading to freedom.

But before we do, we have to set some positive reinforcement ground rules.

First off, this isn't a *dig-up-the-dirt-and-wallow-in-it,* session. And believe me, your agitated soul is going to try to hijack this process the second it gets the chance.

So, let's call it out early, before it tries to call the shots.

Pro Tip: to ensure I didn't turn this into a *beat-up-on-me* session, I started by picking up a thick black marker pen and on an A3 size piece of paper I wrote:

'Only by knowing the source of my agitation can I be free of it!'

A simple reminder to stay vigilant so my agitated soul didn't feed on the memories I was about to exhume.

It also reminded me that my search for the source—the original catalyst that triggered it—was meant to help me surrender it, not identify with it.

Of course, I needed to cultivate its successor as well. But the trick was to make sure they happened in unison: slowly replace one with the other over time.

You see, my mission was for mindfulness to become *instinct* wired into my bones. I knew that would take time and a whole lot of patience, but I was determined to be free of my agitation once and for all.

The problem was, if I did manage to release my agitated soul in any meaningful way, and I neglected to fill the void, it'd sneak right back to where it used to linger.

That's why building a state of *automated, habitual mindfulness* in parallel with the exorcism was vital.

That led me to a second mantra:

'If you refuse to change, you choose to accept!'

This was more a constant reminder that the choice and accountability were all mine. I would no longer blame other people or circumstances for anything.

If you're honest with yourself, as I had become, you'll see it's a dead end. Nothing good comes from blame that no one else will ever hear. It's an endless cycle of disaster.

These mantras became beacons.

They encouraged me to examine the memories and triggers that fuelled my discontent without letting my agitated soul feast on them.

They were also subtle reminders that until that moment, I had been blindly steering through chaos.

It was time to rip the blindfold off.

The First Encounter

With the ground rules set, let's dig in.

Really, how did we get here? One day, we're carefree, happy-go-lucky ankle biters. The next? We're trudging down life's highway with a permanent scowl and a caffeine dependency.

So, what the hell happened? Well, there's only one way to find out: dig deep.

Months of soul-searching sent me on a journey more treacherous than a goat track in a summer downpour. It was an emotional rollercoaster where the hills seemed to rise higher and the plunges drop deeper at every bend.

I'll spare you the sordid details, but when the wild undulations eased, and the shape of the why began to emerge, I came face to face with one unshakable truth: my agitation wasn't just bad luck.

In truth, it was a spicy cocktail of circumstance, misplaced expectations, and an overdose of sheer stupidity, with only a sprinkle of bad luck for garnish.

In the end, that bittersweet awakening exposed a single spark—the moment that lit the fuse. There it was: the source of my agitated soul.

Early Life: Loved but Lost

I was born into a lower-middle-class family, where struggles of daily life profoundly shaped my early years.

Growing up as one of four kids in five years, plus a bonus sibling 15 years later, I often found myself struggling to navigate challenges that came with shared resources and limited means.

Looking back, I often wondered, what life would be like if I'd been born into abundance instead. Would I still have taken the same paths? Would I be burdened with an agitated soul?

Would I possess the battle-weary resilience forged through adversity I have now? It's wild to imagine how social and cultural shifts shape who we become.

Let me be clear: I wanted for nothing. Though my childhood lacked luxury, it gifted me invaluable lessons and traits. Qualities, such as tenacity, respect, loyalty, a drive for perfection, and a strong work ethic, appeared early on.

However, other virtues I now consider just as important, such as gratitude, persistence, perseverance, and a *calm disposition*, were absent.

As a result, over time, discontent became the backbone of my future self.

Deep into my soul-searching, the day eventually came when that single truth hit me like a hammer: my agitated soul could be traced back to a fundamental lack of early success.

Of course, that was just the initial spark. Over time, other ingredients muscled in. It was as if they were enjoying a very long game of *stacks-on-the-mill* at my expense.

But I was confident all other triggers and indicators stemmed back to my lack of success early on.

Why was I so certain? I'm no psychologist, after all. No, but I'm an observer, and this is what I observed in all its simplicity.

When I'm highly agitated, more often than not, after the entire episode has subsided, I find myself lamenting the things I didn't succeed in.

It's as mechanical as clockwork. When the anger burns out, hours later I'm gnawing on bitter memories of past failures; none of them tied to the moment that initially triggered the outburst.

Without signs of early wins to spark motivation, disillusionment creeps in fast. At least it did for me. Unmet self-expectations weigh heavy on a young mind, spawning doubt and uncertainty about one's own potential.

What made it sting all the more was my natural ability. It was evident from a young age I had talent.

One night, my father came home from the pub with some mates and made me stand on a kitchen chair and sing a Connie Francis song. A haunting memory: *talent* implied but rarely spoken of.

I was agile in sport, had musical instinct, was creatively expressive, and I often immersed myself in solving problems that befuddled others. But excellence continued to elude me.

The Paradox and the Potato Chip

I have vivid memories of taking swimming lessons at a young age. I hated them, and often my poor mother had to drag me there kicking and screaming. I can't recall why but I loathed them with a passion.

Then, one day, something happened that flipped everything. At the end of the first week, the instructor produced a bribe, and that bribe changed the game, for me at least.

Most lessons I languished near the rear, not because I wasn't competent, I simply didn't enjoy any part of the experience. My enthusiasm for keeping up with the rest of the class became as waterlogged as my bathers.

That was until the instructor dangled the bait: a bag of potato chips.

The challenge was set. The class was to race across the short side of the pool, and to the victor went the potato glory.

Every week ended with the *chase for the chip*, and I swam like a *Jack Russell Terrier Shark* chasing salt. All week I was sluggish and unbearable, but when the bag of chips materialised, I was bursting with enthusiasm—and first across the pool *every time*.

That first big win, the bag of chips, and the rush of success left its mark. Even now, I can feel it. But it didn't bear much fruit.

It's possible my young brain assumed *winning* would always be this easy. I mean, I won *every time,* and at something I despised, no less.

But here's the rub: back then, I lacked the ingredients that turn wins into wisdom. That chip-fuelled run of wins planted the seed of sky-high expectations and, I suspect, gave birth to my agitated soul.

Without the virtues that convert short-term wins into a lifetime's resilience, I stumbled.

In time, I would come to name them the Paragons of P.

Paragons of P

This is a rare fellowship of virtues whose power lies as much in their alliance as in their individual strength. Together, they elevate effort into something enduring.

Patience – the open hand: trusts the process, allows growth at its own pace, and keeps the heart soft while you toil.

Persistence – the drumbeat: keeps you showing up through daily resistance; the small, faithful unit of progress that survives bad moods and messy days.

Perseverance – the long road: *persistence* over time. Sustains you across seasons and storms with resilience in the face of uncertainty.

Patience steadies the hand so persistence can keep the beat, and together they give perseverance the stamina to go the distance.

Like strands in the same cable, they each draw strength from the others.

As strong as they are, the first three lose their force without the fourth paragon: *purpose*.

Purpose – the compass: stops the other three from becoming brute force without meaning.

With *purpose,* the others gain moral weight. They're no longer just admirable for their grit, but for their alignment to something worth serving.

With purpose steering, and the other three on board, success can endure beyond the first applause.

The Fallout

But that harmony was never mine. Purpose, I had in spades; the other three were missing in action.

And here's the paradox: just as the first three weaken without purpose, it too is hollow without them.

Without the full set of Paragons, later victories never stacked up the same.

I had fallen into the trap of chasing instant wins, and in the process, starved myself of the kind of success that lingers, and unwittingly given rise to my agitated soul.

Today that impatience is evident everywhere. The *right-now* mentality, the never-ending social media *doomscroll,* the next-day delivery culture.

And, if you trace the generational through-line, it's a slippery slope to catastrophe.

From the slow erosion of the *Paragons of P* in my generation, to Gen Z's raw and reactive activism, to Millennials' disillusionment and today's hyper-sensitive impatience, it turns out I was never alone.

It seems we have been building towards this for quite some time. *(Be careful what you wish for, Gen Alpha).*

Naturally, I had other wins, but I lacked the ability to build on them. I had forged an unhealthy expectation of my abilities and of the circumstances that might shape success.

From the Melting Pot into the Cauldron

My parents were very time-poor. Growing up in a household with two full-time working parents raising four chaotic kids shaped a childhood defined by scarcity and love.

They worked their fingers to the bone to give all of us private schooling, a selfless commitment to our future success. However, that sacrifice came at the cost of time and availability, both invisible ingredients of good parenting.

As a result, while I was surrounded by love and support (something that became truly evident much later in life), I often experienced a sense of neglect when it came to guidance and attention.

This absence of parental involvement compounded my feelings of having great potential with no clear direction or mentorship. I felt like a rudderless ship adrift at sea, and it was a lonely place for a very small boy still trying to learn how to navigate solo.

It did, however, deliver unintended perks. Both resilience and self-reliance thrived in me. Yet I was still too green to understand the importance of the *Paragon of P*; that which I needed so desperately to temper my runaway ambition.

As I grew older, my self-reliance emerged as a buoyant force, propelling me toward ambitions that seemed audacious to many.

Paradoxically, the aspiration that drove me to explore paths others might have shied away from only added fuel to the fire of my agitation. Without reaching the level of success I expected, I became more bitter with each passing enterprise.

The melting pot was now a cauldron, and it was reaching boiling point.

Let's see if you can latch on to the pattern here:

The lack of *my* expected success exacerbated my agitation—
which made me more resilient—
which fuelled my passion for greater things—
which drove me towards more lack of success—
which exacerbated my agitation—
which made me more resilient—
which fuelled my passion for greater things—
which ... do you see what I'm getting at?

That fire, the restless pursuit of excellence, should have fuelled growth. Instead, without perseverance, patience, or persistence, it only fanned the flames, hardening my discontent into malcontent.

Ambition without balance is a slow-burning storm. My restless pursuit of excellence quickly became a reckless pursuit of it, and the ramifications began stacking up.

Time and again, for decades, when challenges loomed too large and threatened to overwhelm me, I would abandon one endeavour for another.

All the while, I was simmering in the cauldron, only I *thought* I was taking a warm bath. I was chasing each new adventure with fire, inadvertently dodging the grit required to conquer mediocrity.

The bittersweet irony lay in my abundance of talent across various realms; each skill serving as both a blessing and a curse. I became serviceable and supportive across many fronts but lacked expertise in all of them.

I was destined to lead the life of a *Jack of all trades*, which was not part of my early plan. I desperately wanted to be the master of something, I just didn't know what or how.

The Lure of Something Greater

You know, I've come to realise my constant hunt for new experiences drained my depth of mastery and stole my chance at it.

Looking back, it's as if I perpetually chased every shiny new thing that caught my eye, hoping for satisfaction, but instead, landing deeper in agitation.

I was nothing more than a *serial dopamine chaser*, looking for a quick fix. Could it have been to mask the distinct absence of the Paragon of P?

It was all one big distraction. What I *should have* focussed on was chasing purpose, the compass that drives the Paragon of P.

Instead, I became more and more jaded. I felt like there was no one there to cheer me on. No one to remind me of the skills I was developing.

Even a small but steady stream of *"Hey, you're pretty good at that—stick with it!"* might have made a difference.

Instead, I just ping-ponged between distractions like a hope-fuelled pinball; each shiny new challenge fizzed with promise and obfuscated the path to meaning.

The day I realised I'd become a *Jack of all trades* was an all-time-low for me. It was the furthest thing from what I thought I was pursuing. By then, it felt too late to turn back.

Suddenly, I was the clown in the ring, juggling too many balls. And there's an inevitability to continually adding elements to a juggle; eventually, they all come crashing down.

Yet even the longest road holds a glint of silver; you just have to be willing to see it.

Thankfully I did.

I identified the root cause of my agitated soul.

When that happened, everything began to shift.

It was as if a veil lifted and the fog burned up at dawn, revealing the chaos that had long held me captive in a stark new light.

That shift ignited something deep, and over time I learned to methodically detach from it as a new rhythm of mindfulness took root.

Mindfulness replaced mindlessness, and it didn't distract me, it grounded me. I was no longer chasing the next big thing; I was moving with *purpose*.

Changing my mindset became the key that unlocked the calm I never knew lived within me. That battle was not without its scars mind you, and it wasn't a short war, but it was one worth fighting.

That Which Lurks in the Shadows

It's funny how the world can turn you on your head in an instant. One minute I'm playing tag in the sun with mates, the next I'm locked in *soul negotiations* that could rewrite my entire story.

Sometimes it feels like fate has a twisted sense of humour, watching from the shadows until you look like you have it all under control. Then it unleashes a volley of curveballs.

Understanding lights the path to surrender and the emotional freedom that waits beyond.

I shared my story of agitation to help you stare down your own demons. To spark the courage to hunt the roots of your unease and make peace with this truth: calm and chaos not only coexist, they are inseparable parts of the same paradox. Like the moon cradling the promise of the sun in its glow.

For me, recognising where my agitation began was a pivotal moment; it allowed me to step back and view my feelings from a distance as if they belonged to someone else.

This shift in perspective was liberating. Instead of being trapped by my emotions, I learned to *observe them without judgement*, a non-negotiable skill in the mindfulness playbook.

It's essential to understand that your agitation usually has something important to tell you. It's a rescue flare from an unmet need. Giving it the *right kind* of attention will take you one step closer to being free from it.

You can't surrender your agitated state if you're blind to its origins. Revealing it makes it that much easier.

But, by delving deep into the *reasons*, you can confront that which lurks in the shadows and unravel the complex web of thoughts and experiences that fuel it.

It teaches you to cultivate self-compassion instead of judgement. Eventually, *surrender becomes an act of liberation* rooted in waking up, not giving up.

Ultimately, it's *understanding* that lights the path to surrender and the emotional freedom that waits beyond.

Take your time with this. Don't be in a hurry to find your agitated soul's origins, just be in a hurry to begin. Much of the secret to mindfulness lies in the journey, not in the answer itself.

Give time a chance to nurture the patience and self-kindness in you that's required. You'll be glad you did in the end.

Start by asking yourself a few truth-tipped questions. What were your formative years like? Was your upbringing filled with harmony and warmth, or was it more chaotic and trying?

If you were the youngest child, did you sometimes feel overlooked? Was everyone else too busy with their own lives to notice your needs?

On the flip side, maybe you were the oldest child. Or perhaps you were born with a silver spoon in your mouth.

Were high expectations placed on you that weighed on your shoulders, making it hard to enjoy being a kid? These aren't idle musings: they're breadcrumb trails to the birth of your agitated soul.

Post-Mortem Brutality

So, how about it, *Agitated Soul?* Have you got ideas on where to begin your search? Is your story similar to mine? Maybe perfection was your leash.

Pressure, regardless of form, often creates internal struggle, pushing us to chase an ideal that can feel both alluring and suffocating in equal measure.

Perhaps you've spent countless hours living up to someone else's standard, only to find that the more you achieved, the more agitated you became.

It's a paradox many can relate to.

Having everything yet feeling like something essential is missing, like winning the prize but losing the purpose.

A word of caution: my post-mortem began brutally. I had to constantly remind myself, I was reliving some bitter memories for a very good reason, for emotional archaeology, not for nostalgia.

Our agitated souls cannot be allowed to feed on the memories.

Even now, reflecting on my past sometimes feels like I'm stepping onto a battlefield. Some memories come rushing back with such intensity, it can be both brutal and merciless.

Recollection echoes with the weight of unresolved emotions, and if you're not vigilant, they can pull you back into the vortex of agitation in an instant.

So, before you commence, put some time into your own mantras (or use mine if they resonate with you). Stick them up above your doorway so they're bold, dripping with intimidating kindness, and signed by your soul:

Only by knowing the source of my agitation can I be free of it!

If you refuse to change, you choose to accept!

It's vital that you build an atmosphere of safety first. Prepare your space, your future self will thank you for the welcome mat.

The Soon-to-be-Old You

Permit me to drive this home one more time. By realigning my approach and grounding myself in mindfulness, I discovered the power of *observing my thoughts without judgement*, making space for compassion at the expense of agitation.

Confronting painful experiences is inevitable so it's important not to let feelings of those experiences dictate your present state.

Don't let yesterday's haze rewrite today's forecast.

It might feel a little backwards to revisit the past at first, but that's how forward motion begins. Keep reminding yourself of the objective: to understand *why* you are an agitated soul, so you can surrender it.

Reflecting in this manner is an act of courage that empowers you to confront your inner struggles head-on.

Liberation is letting go and listening to what the pain tried to teach you.

It's giving rise to a harmonious state where the echoes of the past no longer dictate your present or future.

So, take some time to explore your agitated beginnings. Put this book down for a while and spend some quality time with *the soon-to-be old you.*

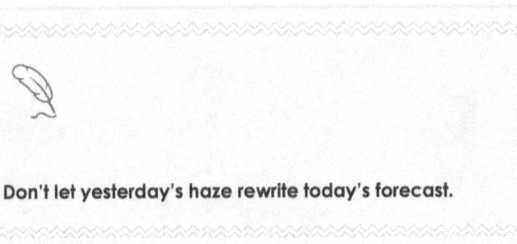

Don't let yesterday's haze rewrite today's forecast.

Most importantly, be gentle with yourself as you go, holding the goal in sight. Freedom from what no longer serves you is on its way. When you're ready, tip your hat to the old self, then let the soon-to-be-new you take its first, sure step forward.

The Calm Amidst the Chaos

5

The Transformation Begins

Now that we've wrestled the soul into honesty, it's time to shift gears and forge the transformation ahead. If you made it through the last chapter without too many scars, well done!

Hopefully, you took your time and faced those demons with curiosity and courage because that's where real growth lives.

I'm not for one minute going to make light of the next steps. I get it; confronting reality can feel like a daunting task, kind of like ripping off the band-aid instead of peeling it away slowly.

But sometimes, stabbing at the heart of the matter is a less painful option in the long run. It opens up so many possibilities for change and improvement.

Let's embrace this fresh start and see where the journey leads.

So, what did the last chapter's exorcism achieve? I have little doubt it unearthed a lot, but did it uncover what you really need?

The primary objective was to find its roots, but the underlying purpose was to give your agitated soul its own identity.

This is a crucial distinction as you're about to see.

Singling out your agitated soul as its own entity allows you to recalibrate your thoughts with more freedom.

It redefines the lines between what you think should change and what you think you should hold on to; the traits worth weaving into your authentic self.

Then, as those traits sharpen *through mindfulness*, you can use them to counter the emotional and physiological signatures of your agitated soul.

Doing so ushers in a gentle, yet firm act of self-compassion.

Remember, the definition of mindfulness is acknowledging your thoughts, feelings, and surroundings *without judgement.*

After the battle lines have been drawn, it's so much easier to let go of the judgement. Suddenly, what once felt overwhelming transforms into something more manageable.

Transformation isn't about discarding who you were; it's about understanding every piece of yourself so you can choose what stays, what evolves, and what is surrendered.

Separation and the Clarity it Provides

Are you beginning to sense the importance of that separation?

Isn't it peculiar, almost whimsical in a way, how the act of letting go, especially of those things we deeply recognise as harmful or destructive, can feel like trying to disentangle ourselves from a thick, sticky web?

Achieving that separation, as difficult as it may be, is a game-changer.

Your agitated soul is no longer an unshakable part of your identity; it's an unwelcome guest that you finally see for what it is. With time, it starts to feel smaller, and you begin to gain the upper hand.

And once you *name it*, its grip slips a little more.

> **Mindfulness is acknowledging your thoughts, feelings, and surroundings *without judgement*.**

Then, the further you venture down the rabbit hole, the more the thought of disassociating from your agitated soul starts to feel appealing rather than foreboding.

That's when the rules of the game turn dramatically in your favour. You can now seize control when the moment presents.

You will cease experiencing life through your agitated soul, and begin to witness it, allowing mindfulness action to slowly take it over.

What a peculiar experience it was. It felt to me like I was sitting in the director's chair on a film set, watching my transformation play out like a cinematic movie of my time on this planet, only at 60x speed.

What happened over years of inner upheaval now looked like minutes of revelation on fast-forward.

This powerful shift releases you to experience life more objectively over time, and that shift sets you free to live with curiosity over control, peace over panic.

Ego is not a Dirty Word

What really helped me connect the dots was recognising this quiet truth: my agitated soul and my ego were not the same species.

Ego was never my enemy. On the contrary, I embraced it at first. My ego—those outward-facing traits—reflected the person I longed to become: my authentic self.

But as agitation crept in, my ego was hijacked. Eventually they were indistinguishable from one another. The ego I once wore with pride, had become unrecognisable.

Hindsight is such a wonderful curse. It's so clear to me now watching that transformation of someone I wanted to be proud of, slowly morph into something I loathed.

But at the time, I wasn't consciously aware it was happening. I just assumed it was a natural evolution in my life.

Before long, my ego became subservient to the agitated force, which was running my life like a chaotic director. And worse, I couldn't break free. How can I break free of something I have no conscious awareness of?

That thought left me wondering: how long had agitation been controlling my ego? Had my outward-facing ego and my inner self been shaped by who I aspired to be, or who my agitation insisted I become?

That was when the question that shattered everything surfaced. Was I truly an agitated soul, or had I simply spent years trapped in a *hijacked ego* that I'd mistaken for something else?

In other words, through years of continual mismanagement of past experiences, had I slowly abandoned my authentic self? I was plagued by that question for some time.

Notice the subtle dance of language unfolding here? Referring to my agitated soul as an object rather than an organic part of my being is a deliberate choice. A fascinating layer of this intricate process of self-exploration.

By distancing my sense of self from this tumultuous energy, I learned to examine it with a curious eye.

It felt like peering into an alien landscape where my emotions morphed into tangibility.

This isn't just semantics; it's a powerful shift in how you relate to yourself and how you better understand your inner complexities.

It allows you to dissect feelings without being overwhelmed, offering deeper insights and revelations about your authentic self, the soul you first set out to be.

And here's the true revelation. Through this lens, you can learn not only to temporarily coexist with your agitation, but also to harness its energy, creatively and constructively, and use it to shape your new narrative.

The Paradox and the Ego

What a breakthrough! It felt like my agitated soul finally declared, *"I'm here! I have my own identity."*

But allow me to be honest; it was pandemonium when my agitated soul threw tantrums because I insisted that my authentic self, be the star of the show, a ludicrous, painfully personal tug-of-war between two inner identities.

Meanwhile, I prayed for a peaceful resolution before becoming the punchline to my own existential crisis.

Eventually, reality set back in, and I slowly realised that keeping the two separated was far easier said than done. It was like debating philosophy with a toddler mid-broccoli protest.

It was positively vaudevillian had it not been so bruising.

There I was, grappling with my own self-worth amidst a battle that some days felt more futile than teaching a cat to fetch a stick.

But perseverance won out in the end and the first fractures began to appear.

They were hairline at first, but they were there.

The barrier that had kept me chained to my agitation was bleeding light through its widening cracks.

I started to hear the soft, persistent whisper of my authentic self, buried deep beneath the cacophony of my agitated soul's relentless demands.

Epiphanies without action, are just poetic illusions.

An inner voice that the clamour of unrealistic expectations and mountains of self-doubt had long muffled.

This authentic self not only yearned a voice but also radiated a long sought after wisdom, stitched from both joyous and painful experience. I never saw *that* coming, but there it was.

It was urging me to embrace vulnerability and authenticity in ways I had once feared, whispering promises of wisdom-fed liberation—if only I dared to listen.

But I couldn't hear that wisdom-fed rallying cry because until that moment my agitated soul was dictating terms.

All I heard, day in day out, was *"We have no tolerance for crap like that because I'm pissed, and everyone's going to know about it!"*

That's when courage stopped being optional.

I knew I had realised something deeply profound, but I had yet to embody it. There was a vast chasm of inertia between the realisation and the intent.

I mean, what's the point of a deep realisation if you don't act on it? It's one thing to see the truth, another to step into it.

Epiphanies without action are just poetic illusions. It was then I realised, I had already begun uncovering deep truths, but until that moment, I had yet to live them.

Courage became the bridge between inaction and commitment, the difference between a fleeting insight and a life-changing transformation.

Fear Nothing, Expect Nothing

There is a soul-bending mantra I want to share. *Fear nothing! Expect nothing!* (or something like that). What an incredibly liberating concept.

I don't know about you, but I came to realise that my agitated soul was 97% fear and expectation in equal parts. When that dawned on me, I knew instantly, my agitated soul couldn't survive without them.

Fearing nothing gives you wings, *and* the sky to fly in. Have you ever truly sat with fear? What part of it is tangible?

I mean what is fear anyway? Is it even real? Or is fear just an accumulation of emotional uncertainty built up across the ages, and peddled by well-oiled propaganda machines?

I mean, most of us live in relatively safe environments, right? So, what is there really to fear? I know I'm over generalising, but it's something to consider as you unpack your situation and circumstance.

What was it that Martin Luther King is often remembered for saying? *"You have nothing to fear but fear itself."* Let that simmer in your subconscious as you read on.

As for expectation, I think I danced with it for far too long.

Suffice it to say, letting it go was my key to freedom; the parachute that brought me safely back.

If you expect nothing, how can you be disappointed?

That revelation lit the fuse, and I finally found the strength to master the art of letting go. I owe so much to that moment in my life. It almost single-handedly rerouted my emotional compass.

That mantra opens the door to the unknown; where possibilities abound, and surprises await around every corner. Where fear holds no leash and outrageous expectation no longer dares to shackle.

It's a rebel's chant to live authentically and unchained.

It made me realise that true freedom lies in relinquishing our grip on what we think should be and instead, embracing simply what is. What a magnificent way to surf the unpredictable tides of existence.

From that moment, a slow burn of enthusiasm grew in me and, as I peeled back the layers of pretence, expectation, and fear, a sense of clarity began to take me over.

A vibrant tapestry woven from passions and desires long hidden, finally basking in their rightful sunlight.

I began to develop a profound appreciation for life's twists and turns instead of meeting them with compounding pessimistic angst.

All of a sudden, *ego* was not a dirty word once more.

I had been given a beautiful reminder that sometimes we must quiet our minds to truly hear our hearts, and in that moment, the transformation began; I was finally on my way.

6

Mindfulness... Meet the Edge of Mayhem

The ego's story stretches through time. It evolved in tandem with our understanding of *the self*. Originally derived from the Latin word *ego*, meaning *I*, it was first popularised in psychology by Sigmund Freud in the early 20th century.

Freud described the ego as one of three parts of the human psyche, the one that balanced out the other two: primal instinct and moral constraint.

Over time, the word ego wormed its way into our everyday chatter, often sprinkled with a hint of disdain.

In casual conversations, the air thickens with judgement as misused iterations of the word *ego* transform it from an intriguing concept into a label for inflated self-worth.

This evolution in language is fascinating; what was once merely a descriptor for one's *sense of self* has morphed into shorthand for arrogance or pretentiousness. It's as if society has collectively decided to wield this term like a dagger against those who dare to shine too brightly, a phenomenon Australians know all too well as *tall poppy syndrome*.

Don't get me wrong, the world is full of *inflated egos* in the literal sense, but is that you? Probably not.

No matter how your agitated soul developed, this story now has three parts: was it by your own hand—a conscious choice—was it your ego, or was it a cry for help from your authentic self, buried deep and aching to be heard.

Slice it how you want—egos are like bellybuttons. Everyone has one, and they all need to be taken care of. A *healthy* ego is essential for personal development and for navigating complex social interactions.

On the other hand, a *well-established* agitated soul is not something to be trifled with. The transition away from it will be slow and delicate, so expect hiccups along the way.

Above all, never underestimate the power your agitated soul has over your ego. There were times I felt like I was David battling Goliath.

But my agitated soul *was* a Goliath; at the peak of its power, taking too long to do up my own shirt left me feeling like I wanted to punch someone. Come on! Really?

Who *is* That Behind the Curtain?

There was another realisation that struck me like thunder rolling across the sky that was just as jarring.

On the inside, my agitated soul was the star of the stage, but when it came time meet the fans at the back door, it sent a proxy: my ego.

Few things are more destructive than an unhealthy soul cowering behind a curtain like an evil wizard.

You know what I'm talking about, right? You're so enraged on the inside that your liver is almost medium rare, but on the outside, you're presenting an icy, *deadpan façade*.

The true destruction here is when it devolves dramatically and the fallout is irreparable.

What I mean by that is, that icy exterior is nearly always reserved for guests only. You know what I'm getting at, right.

Few things are more destructive than an unhealthy soul cowering behind the curtain like an evil Wizard.

We bottle our agitation when we are *out in public* but when we get behind closed doors, it often explodes. And when you live behind closed doors with other people, guess who cops it?

What's worse is that it cycles. It happens over and over again, and we know what happens when repetition becomes part of the formula; it becomes habit, and eventually subconscious.

What a powder keg.

Let's look at it from a different perspective. When the ego is marched to the front lines to *face the public*, why does it put on a front?

Is it trying to protect your agitated soul? Or could it be because the ego is ashamed of what it has sworn to protect?

Both are credible possibilities. But I think it's incumbent upon us to dissect the narrative and work through the detailed machinations. A deepest-level understanding ensures the fixes you're about make are being made at the foundational level. So, keep that in mind as you unpack this.

In my case, my agitated soul became the recluse and *always* sent my ego externally to do all its dirty work. And I'm confident my ego was ashamed of my agitated soul.

Think about the implications here. When I got behind closed doors, the fuse on my emotional *powder keg* was already lit.

So, what's the moral of this story? Well, it's twofold.

Firstly, when we are in an agitated state, the ones we love end up absorbing the shock. That alone should be enough to ignite in you the will to change.

Secondly, what are the benefits of allowing your agitated soul to linger behind the curtain like a worn-out, *egotistical prima donna*? I hope the answer is bleedingly obvious—there are none.

It's emotional sabotage, pure and simple. Suppressing our agitation is a recipe for disaster and we must engineer well-developed mechanisms to vent.

This is an unsettling reminder that true, steadfast courage is rooted in humility, not arrogance. In calm, not in agitation.

And if your agitated soul sends a proxy to give elaborate performances designed to distract those around you from your chaotic tempest swirling within, then brace yourself. Because, in the end, something will change, whether you welcome it or not.

Come Out, Come Out, Wherever You Are

Unravelling the illusion I had built, the distractions masking my restlessness, revealed something far more powerful than I expected: a kind of self-awareness that refused to be ignored.

I must be honest. Embracing this newfound awareness felt like trying to put on skinny jeans after a Christmas lunch. It was very uncomfortable, but it was also necessary.

Think about it. Nobody knows your ego like you do. Actually … scratch that. Nobody knows your ego at all.

You see, despite what I just said, we don't show our ego to the world. What others see is the behaviour that's shaped by it. They're the knee-jerk reactions we fling at life's curveballs when we're on a rant.

Our outward behaviour is just the physical manifestation of our agitated soul's emotional immaturity, at least, mine was. And no, that is not easy to admit, but it is the truth.

Friedrich Nietzsche once said, *"He who has a why to live can bear almost any how,"* which highlights how egos often latch onto purpose for identity.

> I couldn't see my state of agitation until I couldn't stand it anymore.

It's as if our ego acts as a protective shield, shaped by experiences, successes, and even failures that define us. A hijacked ego *pretends to be all that,* whereas our authentic self *is all that.*

Emotional Bias: Naked and Afraid

We all develop emotional biases from our life's experiences. Common in psychology texts, these terms may sound complex, yet the philosophy is quite simple. Think of it like your brain keeping score of your emotional climate throughout your life.

Imagine that each time something emotional happens, you wrote it on a sticky note, so you don't forget the experience.

It might look something like this:

- *When I* **messed up**, *people laughed at me*
- *When I* **helped** *someone, they smiled at me*
- *When I* **was ignored**, *it hurt me*

Over time, emotional biases begin to form around those experiences. They evolve into belief-forming formulas that look more like this:

- *When I* **messed up**, *people laughed at me = don't try hard anymore*
- *When I* **helped** *someone, they smiled at me = helping feels good*
- *When I* **was ignored**, *it hurt me = I must not matter*

Eventually, your brain doesn't necessarily ask if they're true anymore, it just uses your *sticky notes* to make guesses about the world:

- *You think you're bad at something because you* **messed up** *once*
- *You think you're a good person because you* **helped** *someone once*
- *You think you're invisible because you* **were ignored** *once*

Finally, when you believe something emotive before you've really checked if it's true, that belief starts sneaking into your decisions.

It's like sunglasses that tint everything you see, not because the world changed, but because your brain did.

To say my emotional biases were turbulent is an understatement. They began as a slow-building storm but ended in a hurricane.

And here's the brutal truth: I couldn't see it until I couldn't stand it anymore. I think that's worth repeating; *I couldn't really 'see' my state of agitation until I couldn't stand it anymore.*

But I knew early on, it was somehow already reshaping how I saw the world. Each experience fed the emotional bias, and each bias shaped perception.

It's jarring to consider how even a single wound can colour a whole lifetime. It made me realise just how interconnected our emotions and self-identity truly are.

Fess Up, Who Did That?

So, let's talk about you for a moment. Why didn't agitated emotional biases fade in you over time? Why did they grow?

Are you sure you're ready for this?

Because you let it.

There's no way to sugar-coat it. Each and every life experience presents a choice, and we have free will to choose which paths we take.

I have accepted that, despite the difficulties: I am responsible for who I have become. I *chose* that path. I didn't just allow agitation to creep in; I fed it, and so did you.

For me, that was a very bitter pill to swallow, and it wasn't without pain, but eventually, after much toil and grit, things began to feel clearer.

The right path *I had chosen to avoid* lit up like a stage cue I could no longer ignore. And with that light came the first lift of a weight I'd carried all my adult life.

It revealed an unsettling yet liberating truth: I could still retain the essence of who I was without clinging to past constructs that no longer served me.

Just Keep on Punching

Facing my agitated soul meant unravelling beliefs that were tangled with my identity. But finally understanding this journey was about healing, not erasure, gave me courage.

I found comfort in the thought that repairing the damage didn't require discarding everything. Instead, it prompted a thoughtful re-evaluation of what truly mattered and what was worth keeping.

Everything began clicking into place. I embraced the opportunity to become a more *authentic version of myself*. And I did so without *fearing* the loss of who I once was or *expecting anything*—other than change. What a liberating experience!

For the first time in a long, long time, I began feeling comfortable in my own skin once more.

The first breach was done. I had torn through the outer wall of my agitation, and there was no turning back. Now, the only way forward was straight into the *storm's eye*, where calm awaited.

Combatants ... To Your Corners

Let's lighten the mood a little by switching pace.

Before we wind up this chapter, let's look at some practical, every day tools to help you deepen the line in the sand between your agitated soul, your ego, and your authentic self.

These rituals are cheeky and simple, and are designed to be disarming, but real.

They'll help you spot when your ego's being pulled by the wrong master, and give your authentic self the space to breathe while the agitated soul learns to loosen its grip.

Use them in moments when all three start jostling for control.

> ***Pro Tip:*** *Combine these tools with your Mindfulness in Action practices from Chapter 3, and layer them alongside the other exercises you'll meet later in the book.*
>
> *The more you weave them together, the more instinctive they become—like muscle memory for the mind.*
>
> *Over time, you'll notice your ego stepping back, your authentic self edging forward, and your agitated soul hesitating as it reaches for the reins.*

Exercise 1: The 30-Second Ego Check.

When irritation or defensiveness spikes, pause for a micro-reflection:

"Is this my authentic self speaking ... or is the agitated soul throwing a tantrum through its favourite sock puppet?"

This tiny check-in short-circuits reactive spirals before they hijack your day. The more playful you make it, the more disarming it becomes.

Try whispering:

"Authentic Self, I think the agitated soul's throwing its toys out of the pram again. Could you go have a word before the ego builds an impenetrable fortress made from metaphorical Lego bricks?"

Make it yours. Add accents. Use props. The goal here is interruption with a wink so, perfection is not part of the recipe.

Exercise 2: Posture Audit for Emotional Clarity

When you need a sanity check, don't reach for your mobile, reach for your spine.

Stand up. Shake loose. Throw your shoulders back like you're auditioning for *Confident Ego: The Musical.* Hold that pose for 30 seconds.

Now soften everything: jaw, shoulders, belly, stance, the lot. Let your body melt into presence. Hold *that* for 30 seconds.

Which one feels more *you?*

The ego loves to choreograph posture. When the agitated soul has the reins, your body often wears a costume. Unpack the posture, and you'll start unpacking the emotion beneath it.

Bonus Round: try this in front of a mirror and observe the shift.

Name the characters and applaud your authentic self when it finally steps into the spotlight.

Exercise 3: Assign the *Agitated Soul* a Costume and Stage

This might feel strange the first few times, but so did dancing when no one was watching, right?

Humour disempowers *emotional tyranny*. So next time your inner chaos kicks up dust, don't suppress it ... dress it.

Picture your agitated soul being introduced on a prime-time radio game show.

Something like this:

> *"Tonight's guest is wearing a velvet robe over leopard-print leotards, accessorised with a Grateful Dead tee and unmatched Crocs. In its spare time, it enjoys disembarking from vehicles mid-traffic to hurl Latin insults at unsuspecting commuters."*

The more ridiculous, the better. Give it a name. A catchphrase. Add a dramatic monologue.

I can see you now: rolling your eyes and scanning the room for the nearest escape hatch. But hear me out.

When chaos is dressed for comic defeat, it loses its power to intimidate. You stop being *inside* the storm and start watching it from the audience, popcorn in hand, and dignity intact.

Exercise 4: Sticky Note Truth Rewrites

As we touched on earlier in the chapter, your brain's been running a lifelong audit—compiling a *bias* register of your emotional responses.

Every emotional moment—awkward, uplifting, or downright mortifying—got scribbled onto a sticky note and slapped onto the fridge door of your mind.

Over time, those notes stopped being reminders and started becoming rules.

Rules like:

Mistakes = humiliation

Honesty = ridicule

Vulnerability = weakness

They're outdated. They're curling at the edges. They were written through the lens of agitation ... and they're due for a rewrite.

Your mission, should you *choose* to accept it:

Grab a stack of actual sticky notes and write down the raw emotional beliefs that still echo in your decision-making.

They might look something like:

When I spoke up, I got shut down ➔ *speaking up = being shut down*

When I rested, people said I was lazy ➔ *resting = laziness*

When I asked for help, I was dismissed ➔ *asking for help = a burden*

Stick them somewhere visible. On your mirror, your desk, your fridge. Let them stare back at you. Let them speak to you like a guidance counsellor priming you for change.

Then, rewrite them. Not with glittery affirmations, but with grounded truth:

Speaking up = honouring my voice

Resting = restoring my power

Asking for help = connection

This exercise is a reminder of the power your emotional biases hold, both positive and negative.

They turn metaphor into muscle memory, but you can step in and mould them into more positive affirmations; ones that last and grow stronger with time.

You stop responding to triggers automatically and start responding with choice.

Curate the fridge door in your mind. If you don't like what you see, change it.

But you can't change what you can't see. Now they're seen.

And this time, you're the author.

These light-hearted exercises break the ice between stagnation and change. Yes, they're somewhat humorous, but they can have high impact when used well.

They also lay a solid platform for building the strength you'll need when the fight becomes savage.

This last one however, is different. It's not cheeky; it's confrontational.

I'd only recommend trying it when you're in the right emotional state and have the time to sit with it and reflect.

Think of the earlier exercises as shadowboxing.

This is the moment you step into the ring.

Exercise 5: Four Players, One Chair.

It starts, as many things do, with an old truth. It goes like this:

'Before you unleash your anger on someone, write your feelings in the sand.'

The idea being, if you write your grievances in the sand and sleep on it, the tide will come along and wash away any trace of them.

This exercise follows a similar rhythm, but instead of sand, you'll use a journal.

Script a conversation between three voices:

Ego – the protector of *Agitated Soul*, always scanning for threat.

Agitated Soul – the reactor, always looking for a fight.

You – *Authentic Self*, about to begin its rise from the ashes.

Think of this as a test drive. You're not expected to have all the answers, just a willingness to listen, respond, and choose a different approach.

Something like:

Ego: "I'm great thanks, how are you?"

Agitated Soul: "Liar! I'm cracking here. I screamed at a spoon last night."

You: "Can I please just have a little peace and quiet."

Ego: "I don't have the luxury of quiet. I'm trying to put on a show here."

Agitated Soul: "Can we just get this over with and go home."

You: "I don't want to fight anymore."

Be as real with the conversation as you can. Respect the true voice of each part of you.

If the conversation isn't honest, neither will the change be.

When you're in the flow of the conversation, pause for a breath … then *give your authentic voice permission* to speak on your behalf.

It might go something like this:

Ego: "*I think they're buying it. No one seems suspicious.*"

Agitated Soul: "*I couldn't give a flying fingerpainting if they are suspicious.*"

Authentic Self: "*I can't change what others think of me; why give it oxygen?*"

Ego: "*Please! I need to concentrate, or the jig will be up.*"

Agitated Soul: "*Who cares? They're all flogs anyway.*"

Authentic Self: "*Feel the ground holding you. This is where life begins to breathe—now stay here a moment.*"

Giving *Authentic Self* (who up until now has been buried under the stink of *Agitated Soul* and its marionette, *Ego*) permission to step in as proxy, forces *Agitated Soul* to hear a more balanced perspective.

Naturally, the rebellion will be swift and loud, but if you persist, eventually the spell begins to break.

The door for reconciliation then opens and an unspoken pact is formed:

> *it's ok to not let Agitated Soul always have its way.*

Reaching this point is a Herculean effort; the kind that leaves your muscles aching and your mind raw. I know firsthand it's not an easy road to travel.

But once you do, the path ahead feels lighter, and the voice you've just heard will be one you'll want to hear again.

And here's the payoff: writing emotion down turns it into dialogue, and reframes it as drama, not destiny.

You are the seat of power, not convention. Know that. Use it. Keep listening until *Authentic Self* no longer needs permission to speak.

The Calm Amidst the Chaos

7

The Mindfulness vs Meditation Debate

I had never before contemplated embracing mindfulness *or* meditation. Actually, I had always seen them as a lofty, esoteric notion that didn't quite fit my hectic lifestyle or my personality.

To be honest, I figured both would send me straight to sleep. Just picturing myself sitting there in silence, while my brain buzzed with a million thoughts and distractions, felt like a nightmare.

I'd rather be *hugged by a cactus*.

Mindfulness and meditation felt like galaxies away from my chaos. Juggling work, social loops, never-ending to-do lists, and the endless unforgiving craving for creative engagement.

Needless to say, embarking on self-discovery through mindfulness and meditation, was going to be a serious challenge.

Simply put, it was most definitely not my cup of tea, but I felt I had no other choice.

I had painted myself into a corner, and I was sinking fast.

To my surprise, the deeper I dug, the warmer it got.

Finally, I realised that my aversion stemmed more from a pathetic lack of understanding than from any inherent flaw in the practice.

So, I dove in with an open heart and mind, and I quickly discovered the potential for a profound sense of clarity and calm.

I was only researching, mind you, but everything I found challenged my fairy floss assumptions and revealed real potential.

Eventually, it dawned on me that the true test lay not in sitting still but in confronting the whirlwind of thoughts that often clouded my mind.

It was the polar opposite of my ill-informed, preconceived assumptions. Was it really possible that mindfulness and meditation could pave the way to the calm amidst my chaos?

So, I reframed my beliefs through understanding, and in the blink of an eye, that whirlwind of thoughts fast became the centre of the problem, as did the solution.

Running from it was clearly *not* the answer.

To give you some perspective, here's what that whirlwind felt like:

Each thought multiplied, then exponentiated, cannibalising itself in a frenzy of overthinking, then spawned multiple variants of each new exponential thought entanglement.

I was perpetually buried beneath an avalanche of my own mind's making.

How could I not have seen it earlier? The answer was simple: dismantle the machine, or at the very least, tame it. Yeah, right.

It was clear that without taking action, or pausing for reflection, I'd continue sinking in the quicksand of my agitated soul.

More to the point, I would be unable to harness my creativity or make any meaningful advancements in any direction.

So, giving mindfulness and meditation a go was more of a necessary evil than a lifestyle choice.

Yet, uncertainty kept my feet anchored at the starting line, and confusion kept feeding my uncertainty: I couldn't quite grasp the intricate relationship between the two.

Were they one and the same? I delved deeper still, questioning whether mindfulness and meditation were intertwined concepts. Were they fused at the core, or simply two disconnected forces waiting to be unravelled?

Mindfulness: Brewed to Order

Have you heard the saying:

'All thumbs are fingers, but not all fingers are thumbs'?

Let's reframe it. If we give it a twist, we get:

'All meditation is mindfulness, but not all mindfulness is meditation.'

Another way of looking at it is, meditation is one doorway into mindfulness, but mindfulness has many doors.

Let that *simmer for a bit*. Once it clicks, you'll uncover mindfulness techniques hiding everywhere in plain sight. I know it opened my eyes to techniques I would never have considered to be mindfulness prior.

Here's another way to cut it. While many people think of mindfulness as just sitting stiffly in lotus pose, humming enlightenment into the ether, realising its true reach can flip your perception on its head.

It's like discovering your kettle pours any flavour of tea you could dream of.

You could be ploughing through emails, scrubbing pots like you're unveiling ancient relics, or dodging peak-hour traffic, all while being *totally present* through mindfulness.

Mindfulness has been described in countless ways across centuries. I've touched on this many times already. What I offer here is my official definition: *'the art of being fully present and engaged in the moment, without judgement.'*

It's about paying attention to our thoughts, feelings, and surroundings with a sense of curiosity rather than criticism.

Meditation on the other hand, can be thought of as a serene escape from the chaos of daily life. Both require significant practise and commitment to reap their subtler rewards.

In meditation, mindfulness is the constant, hence the analogy, *all meditation is mindfulness*, but they are not interchangeable truths.

Meditation uses technique to coax *stillness*, to sink beneath thought.

Mindfulness, however, is the art of noticing, the *quality of being in the moment*, regardless of whether you are meditating or not.

When you bring the senses into the equation, the difference between the two becomes clearer. Mindfulness is a technique for mastering your senses, while meditation is a technique for detaching from them.

So, while mindfulness pulls us into the *now*, meditation offers a retreat from the *now*.

One grounds us in reality while the other provides a sanctuary away from it when we need it most.

While meditation strengthens mindfulness (training the mind to stay anchored on stillness), it doesn't automatically translate to mindfulness beyond the cushion.

So, while meditating, mindfulness steadies the mind on silence, but outside it, mindfulness lets you steady the mind on anything: a chocolate bar, a breath, an aroma, a rush.

Another important distinction is that meditation typically calls for a still mind *and* body, whereas mindfulness only requires the former.

Many find they can practise mindfulness throughout their day, during meals, conversations, or even undertaking mundane tasks. By consciously directing attention to the experience as it unfolds, they ground themselves in the moment further enhancing life and all it offers.

As you will discover in the next chapter, mindfulness can be practised in the most unexpected environments.

Two Tools, One You

At the risk of sterilising the moment, mindfulness and meditation are tools used for sculpting what's happening on the inside.

They work beautifully on their own, but together, they are unstoppable. When you think about it, using just one tool to tackle a complex task is practically unheard of.

Would a carpenter lean solely on a hammer or a lone saw to build something worthwhile? Would a chef make a crème brûlée with only a spoon and stubborn optimism?

Whether you're cooking dinner, designing rocket parts, or saving lives, impressive results demand tools working in harmony.

How many tools do you use at work? If you're a knowledge worker, chances are your tools number in double digits.

To master any tool in any toolbox takes repetition and experimentation.

So why should inner work be any different? Wouldn't you want optimal conditions when sculpting the new you? It's all about finding that perfect blend of applications and applying each one with intent.

Full Awareness: Your New Superpower

So, what does all that jazz really mean? Here's the secret buried inside it all. Full awareness! It's the golden ticket.

Seriously! When you master the art of full awareness, you're unlocking a secret superpower. You won't have to take my word for it. The proof is in the pudding and you're about to be served.

Mindfulness is the art of noticing. Meditation is the art of surrender.

But before we retreat for dessert, let's dig through this a little more.

Imagine being able to fully enjoy each life experience without distractions or worries. Can you imagine that? Nothing clouding your mind as you immerse yourself in the moment.

When that happens, everything becomes more meaningful.

Colours pop, conversations deepen, and silence starts making sense. Now, how does your storm of agitation look in that new light?

It wasn't until I actually began applying mindfulness, not just reading about it, that I realised its power. It wasn't about achieving some mystical Zen state or silencing my thoughts entirely anymore. It was about grasping the deceptively simple nature of the journey. This was going to be a doddle.

There are only two tools after all, right? And they offer me everything I will ever need, right? How hard could it be, right?

Wrong!

Which brings me to my point: a small caveat, before we charge in.

Don't be like me. Don't expect to flip the euphoric state of wellness on like a light. If you're struggling to read between the lines, I'm trying to ease you subtly into a patient mentality.

Here's how it all panned out for me.

It all began with noticing thoughts, acknowledging their existence, and deciding how much weight they carry. That felt like a simple way to introduce myself. Until I realised how quickly, and often I strayed. Then I knew I was in for a fight.

Despite there being only two tools, you, a heinously complex unit of atoms, are also part of the equation. While the theory is simple, the application is a much bigger beast.

Think about trying to wash the Empire State Building with a bucket and a sponge.

Not to dampen your flourishing enthusiasm but reaching *Zen state* takes time. Even then, it's not going to happen every time you put out the call. Most days, it will be harder to summon than you expect.

But remember my motif from the previous chapter. Sometimes the secret to mindfulness lies in the journey to the answer, not in the answer itself.

Full awareness is potent, though, so it's worth striving for greater and greater returns. It lets you respond with clarity and calmness, not react with your hijacked ego behind the wheel.

It enables you to make better decisions, connect more deeply with others, and cultivate gratitude, turning each moment into a self-fulfilling prophecy.

We've already touched on this but it's worth emphasising: the importance of mindfulness and meditation often gets lost in translation.

Many quickly dismiss it as just a gathering of tree huggers sitting in a circle, harmonising to *Kumbaya My Lord* while sipping herbal tea.

But the reality is far more grounded, intricate, powerful.

That's what makes them matter. They represent a fierce alliance, functioning in symbiotic unity. Each has its own distinct flavour, but together, they're pure *rocket fuel*.

Inner Peace, But at What Cost?

Mindfulness and meditation have been so thoroughly *westernised for profit*, their true benefits get buried beneath the glossy salesmanship.

You know what I mean, those overpriced yoga mats and fancy retreats where you essentially pay to sit quietly in nature.

It sounds lovely but it misses the point entirely.

The wellness industry has exploded into a billion-dollar behemoth. But instead of offering true peace and healing, it plays out like a money-making scheme exploiting our craving for calm.

And it's infuriating (*he spat, agitation bubbling slowly from within*) because the core principles of mindfulness are about finding balance and tranquillity within, not shelling out big bucks for influencer-led classes and shiny branded leotards.

The profit-driven gloss pulls us away from the practices that actually quiet the soul. But when the profit-driven layers are stripped away, mindfulness and meditation can be rediscovered.

Simple yet powerful tools for better living, not just another charge on our subscriptions tab.

Boiling it down, while some people envision Zen masters with long beards floating on clouds, the practices of mindfulness and meditation are about finding calm amidst the chaos of everyday life.

Hopefully, that gives you a deeper understanding of both and how they operate, both separately and together. They're complementary tools, distinct, yet symbiotic, and capable of alchemising your inner chaos.

So, moving forward, let's ditch the stereotypes and embrace the two for what they are: tools for surviving our fast-paced world without completely losing our sanity (or sense of humour).

After all, if we can't laugh at ourselves while trying to achieve inner peace, what's the point? A big part of embracing mindfulness and meditation is recognising that it's okay to be human.

Lean into this journey with a smile and maybe even release a few giggles along the way.

Cracking the Chicken and the Egg Paradox

Philosophers have been debating the *chicken-and-egg question* for centuries.

Paradoxically, mindfulness and meditation fall foul of the same conundrum (pun squarely intended), and cracking open the answer isn't quite as simple as frying up an omelette.

On one hand, you have the egg, which seems to be a prerequisite for the existence of chickens. But then again, without a chicken to lay that egg, how can we have eggs in the first place?

This line of inquiry stirs our fascination with beginnings and underscores life's loopiness.

Pulled into context, the question morphs from *"Which came first, the chicken or the egg?"* to *"Which one comes first, mindfulness or meditation?"*

The chicken and the egg metaphor's a cue that not every question has a clean answer, and sometimes that's perfectly fine. Life is rarely black and white. Sometimes, both truths deserve their own space.

Where To Begin: Wherever You Can

So, which is it, the chicken or the egg? Well, the simple answer is, it really doesn't matter which comes first—as long as one does.

At the end of the day, the goal is to master both disciplines anyway, right?

> You don't need certainty to begin; you just need to begin.

Yes, becoming proficient in both disciplines is the ultimate goal, but because they're neither mutually exclusive nor structurally dependent, it doesn't matter which one comes first.

What does matter is that the very first step is to *start somewhere*, and the very last step is to be *master of both*.

Honestly, I don't recall choosing where to start. Maybe that's because I was working it out as I went. I was coming from a long way back, fumbling my way through moments of confusion, and honestly, it just unfolded organically.

And that, is your third option, which is precisely the point.

You don't need certainty to begin; you *just need to begin*.

You may already be leaning towards one over the other. Perhaps one already feels easy in your mind, while the other feels like wrestling fog.

If that's the case, don't hesitate to follow your instincts. Harness the tailwind of your initial enthusiasm for one over the other.

And there's good reason for approaching it this way.

Momentum Matters

It's your chance to score an early victory or two. Early victories will serve as motivation to build your momentum.

Just like an eager runner hitting the pavement on fresh legs, getting those early yards in while your connection is vibrant, turns motivation into momentum.

It also deepens your understanding and commitment to your overall journey.

Furthermore, it creates a natural evolution to the next step, leveraging what you've learned to cultivate the other.

If you're anything like me, eventually you'll run into the *chasing shiny new things* brick wall.

I remember getting restless earlier than expected (what can I say, it's in my genes), so having a fresh perspective when I needed it was very refreshing.

I wish I could claim to have engineered that leap, but alas, it's all retrospective. Ah, 20/20 hindsight. It's such a wonderful curse.

The Awkward Truth

Before we press on, there's something we need to put on the table: sensitivity.

We're about to tiptoe near the edges of personal territory, so it's only fair to lay out a few guardrails.

The danger in talking about serious topics this broadly is that it can lead to generalisations. But we don't have the luxury of deep familiarity; we're strangers, after all.

So some of this may feel elusive at times. But let's be real: I don't know you from Adam or Eve. And you could say the same of me.

Attempting to diagnose the inner workings of your mind, body and soul here would be reckless (notwithstanding that I'm not qualified to; see the disclaimer in the introduction). So, we'll stick to broad strokes.

That doesn't mean you're off the hook. You're a unique individual with your own mix of needs, just like me.

This is your chance for a raw self-review and an honest re-evaluation of your journey so far; so, I encourage you to take it. Nobody knows you better than you, after all.

And if you'll permit me to poke the bear every once in a while, I promise it will be for good reason. Consider it my cheeky nudge to challenge stale assumptions and dig deeper than surface level.

So, if you're game, let's keep going, broad strokes, bold steps, and a few gentle nudges where it counts.

More Authentic Inking, Less Self Thinking

That said, let's check in. By now, I'm hoping your pages are carrying the scrawl of a short novel.

If they aren't, well, you may just find yourself circling back here. And if repetition's your jam, great. No harm, no foul.

Either way, your notes will shape your long-term success. But your notes aren't meant to be a director's commentary on *my* words. They're meant to be an honest mirror for *yours*.

Personal reflections and raw impressions based on what you're reading. The kind of scribbles no one else could write because they're drawn straight from your own undercurrent.

You can revisit the book as often as you like; it'll still be here. Why waste your ink retelling it? Use that space to chase a deeper truth; the one your agitated soul has been elbowing aside for years.

Lee Iacocca, a titan of the American automotive industry once said, *"The discipline of writing something down is the first step to getting it done."* And he's right. Ideas left rattling around upstairs tend to rot, not blossom.

Pondering endlessly, even obsessively over something, rarely leads to meaningful progress.

Here's something to deliberate: *Twenty minutes of doing something meaningful is more valuable than twenty hours of thinking about doing it'.*

And, once it's on the page, the darkness has one less place to hide.

Not Quite What You Were Expecting, Right

While we're here, let's linger on an old Latin phrase that's echoed throughout centuries: *Temet Nosce* – know thyself.

If you're a fan of *The Matrix*, you might remember it etched above the Oracle's kitchen doorway; a reminder that the hardest battles are fought within.

To me, that's a call to confront what's hiding at the core; the very journey we're about to step into.

Only by knowing thyself can we walk it with real purpose.

Our world is overflowing with distractions and external expectations, so grasping this concept becomes essential for filtering the noise and focussing on what is going to make a real difference.

Know thyself, and let that trust guide you as you feel your way into the process of beginning, like a curious explorer inching into the depths of an uncharted jungle. Ask yourself pointed questions. Know what lights your fire. Understand the catalysts that get you moving.

Just as important, recognise the triggers that throw you off course; the ones that spark procrastination or cloud your clarity.

Here's a test: how long can you sit with your own thoughts before the itch for distraction kicks in?

If the answer is *"not that long"*, you might be better off embracing mindfulness as your launchpad. A few mindful moments here, a quiet observation of breath there.

But if you already find refuge in silence, let meditation be the current that carries you forward.

Twenty minutes of doing something meaningful is more valuable than twenty hours of thinking about doing it.

Ultimately, knowing yourself is about honouring where you are right now and using that understanding as a compass to guide you.

Just Get Started

So, whether you choose the chicken or the egg, remember, there *is* no right answer other than getting started.

The journey of self-discovery is deeply personal, and finding the right fit is part of the work.

And let's be clear: these two aren't your only options. Do some research, find other tools or techniques that resonate with you, and maybe start there.

Either way, just get started. Channel your enthusiasm; it'll make the next steps feel less steep. Take longer strides from the get-go and you'll feel like you're walking on stilts, not hot coals.

Look for those bursts of zeal and slingshot from them. You'll find your groove soon enough.

Embrace the uncertainty too. It's not a flaw; it's part of the journey. Every expert was once a beginner, and those first awkward moments pave the way for experience and maturity.

So, don't let fear hold you back. The excitement of uncharted territory far outweighs the discomfort of stepping outside your comfort zone … if only you dare.

Above all, celebrate small victories. They'll fuel your motivation and keep that fire burning bright.

So take a deep breath and jump right on in. Trust yourself to navigate what's ahead and remember: you are capable of far more than you realise.

The Calm Amidst the Chaos

8

Embracing Mindfulness and Meditation

Embracing mindfulness and meditation can be as simple or as gloriously convoluted as you care to make it.

In its most elementary form, meditation simply requires you to sit down, close your eyes, and try not to think about how many snacks there are in the pantry.

Sometimes it can be less like serene enlightenment and more like a mental game of hide-and-seek with your thoughts.

The problem is your thoughts are like sneaky little goblins that keep popping up and scaring the bejeebers out of you just as you're about to fly away on a cloud.

As for mindfulness, it doesn't require a mountain-top retreat, or a mystical figure named *Breathe-O* in flowing linen robes.

Nope. You can do it in your pyjamas while binge-watching your favourite show if you really want to.

That's the beauty of it. Everyone finds their centre in wildly different ways.

In a previous chapter, we explored how mindfulness and meditation dance together like a well-worn pair of tap shoes. Meditation is the escape, while mindfulness keeps us grounded.

This chapter aims to disentangle them to get a cleaner grasp of each. Let's begin with meditation.

There are several different environments in which I get meditative traction, but my favourite by far is behind the drum kit.

Yes, you read it right. Pounding along to my favourite songs blasting on volume 11 ushers me into a serene meditative state others find with a scented candle and silence.

Now, that may sound counterintuitive because stereotypically, loud noises and meditative states are not considered conventional bedfellows, but it works for me.

Having spent the majority of my adult life as a professional musician, music is now stitched into the very fabric of me. It's as essential to me as breathing.

From the moment I could first tap my toes to a beat or hum along with a tune, I've been entranced by its power and beauty.

And it's those two specific facets of music that, for as long as I can remember, have captivated me endlessly: groove and melody, though not necessarily in that order.

How Deep is the Pocket?

When I play, part of the process is practising my craft, but I'm also seeking the centre of the groove in a song, often referred to as *the pocket* in the industry. That's the meditative aspect.

A lot of the time, I tend to play *around the edge* of the pocket, but my aim is always to find its centre.

As I drift towards the centre of the pocket, a sense of nothingness creeps in and the closer I get, the more it intensifies.

In those scarce moments when I do arrive right at its centre, it's as if time stands still. The world around me fades away, and all that exists is my authentic self and that groove.

This is rare air indeed, my friend. In a heavy session I'm lucky to sit right in the pocket once or twice, and even then, it's rarely for more than 30 seconds.

The rarity used to frustrate me endlessly, until I realised my agitated soul was behind the noise. The more progress I made, the less frustrated I became, and the more joy I found in the search itself. Now that's a paradox worth beating a drum to.

The playing becomes an extension of my emotions, a dialogue between me and the groove. When I eventually sync with the pocket, a profound connection forms.

And what do I find there? A deep calm amidst my chaos, where my mind finally quiets, and agitation dissolves. The entire experience is positively transformative.

Remember, mastery doesn't come overnight. However, actively engaging in meditative practice always brings something valuable from every session. Sometimes it's more patience, other times it's less agitation, or even clearer thought. There's always payback.

It also brings things like broader limb awareness, or a deeper feeling of limb syncopation. That's the mindfulness side of the coin, which we'll get to later.

My intention with each session is to ease my mind into a blissful state of flow and let the outside world fade away, but it doesn't always go to plan.

And chances are, your chosen path will misfire too, sometimes. Learning to deal with the hits and misses is a big part of it.

But that's life, right?

For the most part, however, before long, I no longer hear the *noise*; I drift away on the groove, which heightens my meditative state.

The longer I sit in or around the pocket, the more intense the meditative state feels, and the more the groove draws me in.

It's no exaggeration, it's *soul-level therapy*.

I could put on a click track and drift away inside John Bonham's *Fool in the Rain* groove forever. It feels like I get lost yet found at the same time, and it's a journey I'll never tire of.

Too Small for Thought, Too Big for Words

Similarly, drifting away on Karen Carpenter's rich, dulcet tones in *We've Only Just Begun*, or when k.d. lang sings *Hallelujah* or *Constant Craving*, draws me into that suspended, timeless space.

In those moments I fall into the same meditative state I inhabit when I'm hunting *the pocket*, despite the pathways being outrageously different.

It's not the song mind you, it's the melody itself, and the gorgeous, rich textures and nuances the voice pours into it.

There's something there that I can't quite put my finger on. But here's the paradox: whatever *it* is, it's so intricate, so *sub-atomic* that there is only room enough for *it*—and *it* alone—in my mind.

It's as if *it* demands the totality of my mind's vacuum for it to resonate, and when it does, that's when I feel the presence of *Authentic Self*.

I want to point out that I am not just killing time here, far from it. I'm using a great melody, or a *kickass* groove to train my brain to focus on something deeply personal to me.

And it works too, *gosh darn it*. No words quite capture that feeling of pure *presence in the moment*.

My musical experiences are personal revelations that cannot be conveyed through mere words. They're profound, personal encounters that shape the way I tune into my own creative pulse.

As Morpheus told Neo after he took the red pill *'No one can be told what The Matrix is. You have to see it for yourself'*, the same is true here; you have to *feel it*.

And when you do, you'll find yourself on your own quest for self-discovery, whether through music, writing, visual art, or any other muse just waiting to be discovered.

Finding Meditation in Most Unexpected Places

My good friend fixes bikes to achieve similar meditative depth.

You've got to think laterally and break out of the dusty stereotypes of what meditation *should* mean. Begin with things that interest you, or you like to be involved in. Just keep looking until you find the methods that fit.

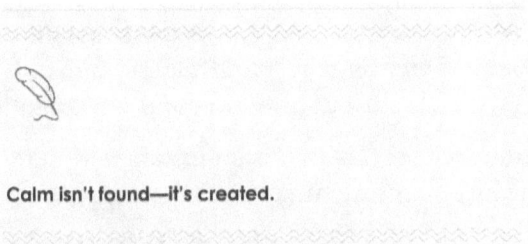

Calm isn't found—it's created.

When you find what works, over time, it'll unleash a torrent of meditation practices that dissolve barriers between your thought and spirit—that's the key.

Like *Happy Gilmore*, you must find your happy place, and odds are, it won't be what you first imagined. (Funny, I've just realised, he might be *the* agitated soul poster boy.)

Once you've found it, guard it. Set yourself up to thrive. Build a space that invites focus and flow and keeps the noise at bay.

Because, if you don't, you're on a hiding to nothing. As sure as dive-bombing magpies in spring, just as the stress starts to melt away, the Seventh Day Adventists prowling the hood will ring your doorbell and crash the party.

Create that space and treat it with respect, especially early on.

There are more ways I use to sink into meditation, but for now, I hope you've got enough spark to start weaving the practices into your daily life.

True focus isn't just about concentration; it's about embracing the catalyst (in my case, the melody or groove of a song) for a deeper exploration.

From Flow to Focus: The Mindfulness Shift

Let's turn our minds to mindfulness (pun paradoxically intended). Practising mindfulness solo does raise the bar, but it's far from counterproductive, it just takes a little more intention.

In a world drowning in distractions, it's all too easy to be pulled under by the chaos of our thoughts or the constant onslaught of external noise. Which is why mindfulness demands our active participation; it calls for our attention and our intention.

True mastery is the ability to summon that state anywhere, anytime, in any environment, without the support of meditation.

Right now, with drumming, I'm not there. For me it's still a meditative practice, a way to clear my head of everything except *the pocket*.

But being in a mindful state while playing is the pinnacle; one I know might take years to reach without the meditative crutch.

So, for now I treat that meditative lock as a stepping stone towards a place in time when I'm *living* in the groove rather than being lost in it. And when I feel the need to step into mindfulness more deliberately, I change tack, turning to simpler activities. High on that list is cycling.

Mindfulness in Motion

When I ride a bicycle for leisure, mindfulness takes the lead. Early on I had to work for it, but now it comes very naturally.

As we've touched on, mindfulness is about being *deeply present in the moment without judgement*. Feeling the cool bite of morning air in your lungs, the shards of dusk sunlight through the gum leaves, the distant laugh of kookaburras.

Combined, they create a symphony of sensations that can awaken your senses and draw you in to the now.

These days I feel like I ride with a mission to fully inhabit the present moment. A purposeful choice to let the ride's rhythm take over.

When it does, the static of worry dissolves, clarity gathers in its place, and with every turn and incline comes new invitations to *be present*.

Riding often reminds me that life's journey is about experiencing each moment, not just landing at a place in time. I'm not focussed on *arriving* anymore.

Steven Tyler, lead singer of American rock band *Aerosmith*, said it best: *"Life's a journey, not a destination."*

This deep engagement exemplifies what mindfulness embodies to me. Anchoring myself in the present, allowing the rhythm of my breath and the cadence of my pedalling to ground me.

Each element: the rustle of leaves, or the distant sound of flowing water, elevates my awareness and reinforces my connection to both nature and me.

Are You Living, or Merely Existing?

Let me paint you a picture: you've just wrapped up a long day at work, and as you slide into the driver's seat of your car, the weight of the world settles on your shoulders.

You turn on the engine and embark on that familiar 45-minute commute home.

You navigate complex traffic patterns, dodge erratic drivers, and even sing along to your favourite tunes. Then, when you finally pull into your driveway and sit back in disbelief, you mutter *"Damn! How did I get here?"*

You just performed all the complex motor skills needed to control a one and a half tonne machine.

What's more, you used them non-stop for 45 minutes, navigating through hundreds of different and sometimes unique experiences, without being consciously aware of a single one.

Yet, there you sit, 45 minutes later, wondering if *Scotty beamed you up*, gobsmacked that you can't remember a single moment of the drive home. How is that possible? More importantly, why does it happen?

**Mindfulness is a technique for mastering your senses.
Meditation is a technique for detaching from them.**

It happens because, in those moments of automatic mastery, while you're *driving*, your instincts are taking charge.

On the surface, it's a beautiful dance between skill and subconscious flow that makes every journey a streamlined one.

The reality, however, is much more sombre. When we let our instincts run the show, we are robbed of existence.

Now, that may sound a tad melodramatic to you, but that is the realisation we all must face.

It's *the Coffee Conundrum* all over again—the cup is empty and not one memory of consuming it. That drive home was 45 minutes invested *not in the present*.

Hang on, that can't be right! The present is where life actually happens, right? And that's precisely my point.

This isn't just a quirky tale, it exemplifies why mindfulness is essential in our fast-paced lives. Mindfulness helps us reclaim those fleeting moments that slip through our fingers unnoticed.

It transforms mundane commutes into meaningful opportunities for reflection and gratitude, allowing us to savour life rather than merely exist absent-minded within it.

Embracing mindfulness means actively engaging with each moment, rather than letting life pass us by in a blur.

Consider how different your commute could be if you approached it with mindfulness.

Instead of immersing yourself deep in your negative thoughts (and let's have brutal honesty here, most of us do it most of the time; that's *why* we're agitated souls), you could *choose* to focus on your surroundings.

The colours of the trees, the architecture of buildings, or even your breath as you drive. Your life is not playing out in your mind; it's playing out around you, so live it.

Whenever I reflect on this example, I'm reminded that mindfulness is a *way of living*. It's an active choice to engage with each experience wholeheartedly.

Noticing how nature's colours shift from street to street, or revelling in the freedom of riding a bike downhill with the wind in your face. Every detail should remind you how much joy there is to be had in *the present*.

Are you truly living, or are you merely existing? That's a sobering thought, wouldn't you say?

The Stars of the Show

Is the distinction between mindfulness and meditation becoming clearer to you? More to the point, are you beginning to appreciate what they can do and how they work together?

As you explore their differences, it's important to recognise the unique roles each practice plays in nurturing your well-being.

Sometimes, you'll need mindfulness to heighten your awareness of your thoughts and feelings in the present moment.

Other times, you may need meditation for a deeper moment of introspection because you're struggling to disconnect from the noise of daily life.

Rest assured, whichever you call on, they both show up.

I have this weird pantomime analogy about their relationship. Picture this: mindfulness and meditation are the stars of the Broadway musical *'Phantom of the Ashram'*.

They both hit the stage together, every time, yet each knows intuitively when it's time to step into the spotlight.

When I'm drumming, meditation takes centre stage, guiding me into a blissful state where my thoughts quiet down and I ease slowly into *the pocket*.

Meanwhile, mindfulness is content in the ensemble, ensuring I remain present and engaged enough to settle into that rhythmic sweet spot.

It's magical how this connection works; my conscious thoughts fade, yet I'm still able to drift toward *the pocket*. That tells me that mindfulness is in play, even if only to a small degree.

In contrast, when I'm riding, or mowing the lawn for example, I enter a deep state of mindfulness, completely immersed in the present. Yet the rich sensory flow invites a gentle meditative undercurrent, showing that meditation, too, is quietly present.

Where are the Stars of the Musical?

But sometimes I struggle to achieve either, my agitated soul overwhelms them both. That's when the flood gates open, reality charges in, and all hell breaks loose.

Thoughts race in like they're competing for gold medals in the *Anxiety Olympics*, and before I know it, I'm contemplating whether my cat is plotting world domination when all I really want is ten minutes of dedicated *me time*.

If it weren't so destructive, it would be comical how quickly serenity can devolve into mayhem. Hence, finding that sweet spot is essential before you go from *om* to *oh no!* faster than you can say *namaste*.

Reality has a funny way of crashing the party and pulling us back into the whirlwind, doesn't it? And herein lies the heart of it all: embrace those fleeting moments of calm amidst the chaos.

That statement challenges the belief that rigid routines are the only path to personal growth, arguing that true mastery lies in understanding and adapting rather than conforming.

You don't need incense, a yoga mat, or even silence. All you need is you.

It's a potent reminder that joy isn't reserved for the extraordinary; it can be discovered in the most ordinary places if we choose to look closely enough.

See, life isn't so complicated, is it?

By shifting from rigid routines to fluid experiences, you open yourself to a richer tapestry of life where joy thrives with simplicity and authenticity.

No Rules, Just Reconnection

At their core, mindfulness and meditation are all about presence. Whether you're stretching in your living room, cycling through a mid-summer breeze, or sinking into the groove of a tune, every experience is an opening to return to yourself.

You don't need incense, a yoga mat, or even silence, just a willingness to meet yourself where you are. No rules, no pressure.

Follow along to an online video, crank up some music that gets your heart pumping, or listen to what your body asks of you in that moment.

Get creative. Perfection isn't the point. Feeling good and letting go is. And in the end, that's the art, right? Showing up for your own life exactly as it unfolds.

Calm isn't found—it's created.

9

Practising Mindfulness and Meditation

Philosophy inspires, but action transforms. So far, we've explored mindfulness, meditation, and the layers of agitation. We've also mapped the mental terrain shaping your inner world through a philosophical perspective.

Yes, we've *dabbled* with practical applications along the way, but now it's time to move well beyond theory. It's time to practise.

A grounding thought before we get practical. *Best practice* in any craft is fuelled by powerful philosophical insights.

And philosophy does more than frame practice, it steels it. It's the quiet breath before the plunge, the scaffolding that holds the lights, the resonance in the space between words.

If a good bit of *sturdy scaffolding* is your thing, go and download my *Ten Commandments* tool from the website. They're universal disciplines that can support any moment, mood or mental state.

Feel free to reference them as we progress through this chapter.

There's also a subtle but important distinction I want to make as we ready ourselves for both practices.

When it comes to meditation practices, your subconscious mind is engaged, and your focus will be turned inwards.

As for mindfulness, your conscious mind takes the lead, and your focus will be directed *out* into the world around you.

Okay, let's channel these abstract ideas into tangible tools that will embed presence, clarity, and resilience into daily life.

Let's tackle meditation first. Are you ready to begin?

Perfect Practise Makes Perfect Meditation

To amplify your mindfulness practice, consider these deceptively simple steps.

Don't panic, you won't have to tie yourself into a pretzel and levitate for an hour. They're so common sense, they make breathing look complicated.

Find a quiet, comfortable space where you can focus without distractions:

To maximise your mental clarity, it is essential to find a quiet and comfortable space that serves as your personal Zen zone. It should be free from distractions, allowing you to immerse yourself slowly in gentle attention.

Over time, this space will be used for more than just quieting the mind. It will become the birthplace of clarity.

Clarity forms the foundation of both deep relaxation, and razor-sharp focus. You'll need skills in both whether you're meditating or tackling the chaos.

Make it a habit to return to this sanctuary whenever you feel the need to be in a deeper state of focus and creativity.

Consider the importance of sensory elements in this space; soft lighting, calming colours, and comfortable furniture can enhance your ability to relax and concentrate.

By prioritising this space, you are actively creating an environment that provides the conditions for mental agility.

And while productivity is not the goal here, don't be surprised when deep focus spills over into everything you do.

Embrace the power of a dedicated Zen zone; it's not a luxury! It's a necessity for anyone serious about protecting their mental well-being. Build it, protect it, and feel it flow.

Start with short sessions to build your meditation muscles:

Building a peaceful mind is a gradual process that requires dedication and effort.

"Patience is bitter, but its fruit is sweet," wrote Rousseau. Give the fruit of your patience time to ripen. Starting small with short meditation sessions is both practical and essential for developing mental resilience.

This incremental approach helps cultivate your *meditation muscles*. Think of meditation as mental strength training, enabling you to increase session length as your comfort and confidence grow.

Start with just a few minutes a day and allow each session to build endurance. Soon, the effort that once felt uncomfortable will become second nature.

Embrace these initial short sessions with determination, knowing that each one lays the foundation for mindfulness and meditation in your life. With consistent practise, you will transform fleeting moments of calm into a sanctuary of enduring serenity.

Remember, good things take time, and transformation is a very good thing. Treat tranquillity like a mosaic; each short session lays another tile.

Focus on your breath to keep you rooted in the present moment:

Focussing on your breath is a powerful anchor for meditation, keeping you firmly rooted in the present moment.

In an age of restless attention and constant demands, harnessing the simple act of breathing allows you to repossess your presence.

Here, mindfulness steps back into the ensemble leaving meditation to grab the limelight. It helps you stay present while meditation deepens the connection within.

For some, focussing on breath alone is enough. Others find it helpful to add a mantra, a steady rhythm to reinforce focus.

Monks in Tibet chant *Om*, a sacred sound believed to harmonise mind, body, and spirit. Chanting *Om* aids in the reconnection to the universe by providing a point of mental concentration.

The repetitive nature of the sound acts as a mental anchor, guiding attention away from distractions and towards a state of inner stillness. The resonance soothes the nervous system and invites a deeper mental quiet.

If chanting *Om* feels a bit too *mystical* for you, spice it up a bit, as long as it's repetitive and monotone, it can have a similar effect.

A mantra I like to use is:

> *"Breathe in the good shit, blow out the bullshit".*

But hey, find what works for you. Chanting is particularly beneficial for auditory learners.

> Meditation isn't about eliminating thoughts; it's about mastering your response to them.

Visualise your breath however you see fit. For me, each inhalation brings in clarity and energy, while each exhalation releases tension and chaos.

Inhale sunlight, exhale storm clouds.

It exemplifies a harmonious balance within. You remain grounded regardless of external chaos. Don't think of it as merely an automatic function but rather as a deliberate tool for cultivating self-awareness.

Don't stress about clearing your mind completely:

Be a pragmatist. Clearing your mind entirely is a noble and worthwhile pursuit. But even Tiger Woods didn't pick up a driver for the first time and knock it 300 metres down the middle of the fairway, right?

Okay, maybe *he* did. Still, treat meditation the same. It's about the swing, not the distance.

Recognise too, that thoughts will inevitably arise. It's a normal part of the process. The misconception that a perfectly still mind is the only way, just leads to unnecessary frustration.

Instead, embrace the fact that your thoughts are a natural occurrence. But when they do arise, gently redirect your attention back to your breath or a specific point of focus.

This builds patience and strengthens your ability to stay focussed when faced with distractions.

Recognition is a crucial step in regaining your focus. If you encounter unusual levels of internal distraction, acknowledge the presence of each, one at a time.

Once you have identified the distraction, allow yourself to *observe it without judgement*, like watching a bird take flight.

Visualise it soaring away into the vast expanse of the ether, gradually fading from your mind. This helps you distance yourself from the distraction so you can redirect your attention back to the task at hand.

Empower yourself to engage more fully in each moment without falling into the trap of self-judgement or entertaining anxiety associated with wandering thoughts.

Meditation isn't about eliminating thoughts; it's about mastering your response to them. Accepting them, releasing them, and stepping into the clarity.

Explore meditation techniques that work for you:

Meditation isn't one-size-fits-all. What calms one mind might bore another, so the key is experimentation and finding techniques that click with your unique rhythm.

Dedicate some time. Every method you explore will bring you one step closer to mastering meditation *your way*. When you find what resonates, then the transformation begins.

Consistency is key:

Consistency is the bridge between effort and transformation. Meditation is less about occasional deep dives and more about steady, daily steps.

Even just a few minutes each day can reshape how you think and feel. It's not the duration but the regularity that shapes the habit. Consistency compounds the benefits.

As you make meditation a non-negotiable part of your daily routine, you will begin to see dramatic improvements. You'll notice heightened awareness, increased resilience, and improved emotional regulation in daily life.

The transformative power of consistency cannot be understated; small efforts repeated day after day can yield profound changes in your mental landscape.

Believe me; conquer this and your future self will send you thank you cards.

Be patient and kind to yourself:

Meditation is a practice, not a perfection. The path is filled with ups and downs, and expecting flawless execution from the start will only leave you feeling frustrated and disappointed.

Even wandering thoughts aren't failures but rather natural occurrences that everyone experiences. Each time your mind drifts, it's a chance to strengthen your awareness, like steering a ship back on course. Think of every correction as progress.

Meditation is about learning to *sit with* your mind, not silence it. To guide it and to grow with it. Just relax, breathe, trust the process, and let your inner Zen master shine.

Remember, every time you sit down to meditate, you're taking another step forward. Even a *restless session* will leave you better off, so honour your efforts and celebrate each victory along the way, no matter how small.

Mindfulness Over Matter

With practical meditation techniques now under our belt, it's time to turn our focus to their equally powerful counterpart: mindfulness.

The two share deep synergies—that we've well and truly unpacked already—yet it's the *intention* behind each that sets them apart.

Meditation gives you a defined inner container for stillness and inward attention. Mindfulness, by contrast, dissolves that container, inviting you to inhabit the present moment in the thick of your everyday life, *without judgement*.

In the pages ahead, we'll explore a series of practical mindfulness approaches. Some echo the meditation practices, while others open entirely new doorways into presence.

Each has its own purpose and intent, and together they'll give you a richer, more integrated way to blossom.

Let's break them down:

Pay attention to your breath:

Before you can meet the present moment, you have to notice it, and nothing invites you there more reliably than your breath.

This steady, constant rhythm draws awareness inward while rooting you in what's unfolding right now.

Giving it your full *conscious* attention, lays the foundation for every other mindfulness practice, strengthening your connection to *what is* with each inhale and exhale.

Follow the rise and fall, the rhythm and flow, until you feel yourself settled. From that still point, let your awareness expand, first to one sense, then another, easing gradually into the full spectrum of presence.

Let the heightened awareness that follows take you above the noise, anchoring you in calm, even amidst the chaos.

Personally, I begin with sound. Maybe it's the years of music training (I should be deaf by now, actually), or maybe it's just the one sense I can fully isolate. With eyes closed and touch, taste, and smell on pause, my ears sharpen.

Whichever sense you choose, let the breath be your constant. Build your awareness layer by layer until every sense moves together in complete, mindful harmony.

Practise deep listening:

Deep listening is essential to effective communication and building strong relationships. It demands full presence in conversations without judgement or interruption.

It shows great respect for the speaker but also fosters an environment where ideas flow, leading to more meaningful exchanges.

When you give your full attention, you start hearing what's felt, not just what's said. It rewires instinct, replacing knee-jerk reactions with thoughtful and considered replies.

It also builds a richer, more reliable knowledge base allowing us to connect with others on a more profound level. We begin to set aside our biases and ego, and build dialogue from shared truth, not assumed certainty.

Ultimately, embracing deep listening turns conversations into powerful opportunities for connection and growth. It also strengthens your ability to slip into a mindfulness state with greater ease.

As your conversational interactions deepen, let that same awareness ripple outwards to the world around you. You'll hear birds the way you've never heard them before. Traffic noise will take on a whole new dynamic. Even the sound of silence changes.

The deeper the listening, the richer the life that gets woven around you. Silence, sound, presence, conversations, relationships; they all expand.

Observe your surroundings:

Building on the previous discipline, to truly engage with the world, begin by *seeing* it differently.

Don't just look; *observe* with fierce intent. Strip away assumptions and meet the moment with open eyes. Set aside labels and invite the moment to open itself to you *as it is*.

Don't see it as you *expect it to be*.

This is positively transformative, but only with patience. And that's the game, right? We're playing in Zen master territory now.

If you can transcend merely living to truly *existing*, even the chaos of rush hour becomes a tapestry of colour and motion. A gentle reminder of the constant movement and change of life, rather than a visual assault.

Observation with intent deepens our appreciation for long-forgotten intricacies of daily life.

The deeper you observe, the more reality unfolds until every moment, every detail, feels woven into something far greater than you've ever thought possible.

Engage in mindful eating:

Mindful eating cultivates a deeper connection with food, strengthens our appreciation for nourishment, and enhances our overall dining experience.

Paying close attention to the flavours, textures, and sensations in each bite nourishes our bodies, and each pause for reflection, betwixt one taste and the next, enriches our minds.

This practice demands that we slow down during meals, allowing ourselves to fully savour the moment instead of rushing through it.

When we focus on what we're consuming—the crispness of fresh vegetables, or the richness of a well-cooked sauce—we become more attuned to our body's hunger signals and emotional responses.

Many Eastern cultures eat food with their hands. It is considered more intimate and connected to the food being consumed, allowing for a more sensory experience.

It's also believed to enhance the flavours of the food as the heat and oils from the hands can add subtle nuances to the taste.

Research has identified that eating with our hands can heighten sensory awareness and foster greater presence during meals, making us more attuned to the act of eating and the sensations it evokes.

Have you ever caught yourself out, chewing mechanically on dinner, your mind racing? You're miles away, processing every conceivable thought; *everything except the food you're eating?*

Your fork is already loaded with the next bite, ready to go, and you haven't even commenced chewing the current bite?

That's not eating! That's autopilot, and if that's you, it's time to stop—really.

Think about the madness of that for a second. That food becomes your future self, yet we dismiss it like an afterthought.

Isn't it time we started treating food like nourishment instead of fuel?

Mindful eating empowers us.

In that state we begin *to actually taste food* (here we are, back at the coffee conundrum yet again), and that encourages us to make healthier choices.

It leads to greater satisfaction, possibly even with smaller portions. Ultimately, embracing this discipline transforms eating from a routine task into a fulfilling ritual that honours both our food and us.

Practise gratitude:

Gratitude is not just feel-good fluff; it's a transformative tool.

Regular reflection and deep appreciation for life's positive aspects, sharpens the habit of focussing on what truly matters.

Acknowledging even the simplest joys, be it a warm cup of coffee, a kind word from a friend, or the complex beauty of nature, can melt agitation and deflate negativity.

The intentional act of gratitude replaces automated patterns of negative behaviour with perspective. It opens us up to recognise blessings that oftentimes go unnoticed.

Set aside labels and invite this moment to open itself to you as it is.

Gratitude also strengthens relationships without effort because it creates an environment where positivity thrives for you and for others. It exudes connection and appreciation and enriches our lives immeasurably.

Embrace mindful movement:

Mindful movement is a gateway to a deeper connection with your body, breath, and presence.

We touched on this earlier in Chapter 3 with *'The Dance & Detox Combo'*, but it's worth revisiting here.

Deliberate *mindful* activities such as walking, yoga, or tai chi, tune you into your movement's natural symphony, returning us to a presence often lost in modern haste.

It tones the body, steadies the mind, and grounds the emotions.

Over time, you learn to recognise how various movements affect your mood and energy levels. Each stretch, step, and twist, when done in *mindfulness*, transforms the mundane into sacred movement.

It's relaxing, de-stressing, and it strengthens you from the inside out.

The more tuned you become the more other aspects follow into mindfulness: better posture, more natural alignment, even weight distribution, and greater balance. All of which help prevent injury and enhance performance in other physical pursuits.

The practice of mindful movement will enrich your years but more importantly, it will extend them.

Putting that another way, prioritising mindful movement over *exercise* is not just about longevity, it's about living fully, vibrantly, and in sync with your body's wisdom.

Don't think about your overflowing inbox, or even your mortgage; it's not the right time. Pay attention to the vessel that carries you through this life.

It's more important than you acknowledge, and it can teach you more than you know. So listen to it.

Open the Door to Present Moment Awareness

So, there you have it. The disciplines of both meditation and mindfulness, all of which lead us to the ultimate goal: cultivating *deep, present-moment awareness.*

Meditation lays the foundation for training the mind to be still, intentional, and aware. Mindfulness dovetails with meditation and expands the result by making our sensory receptors become hyper-sensitive to *this* moment.

Mindfulness carries *presence* beyond the cushion, giving you the power to embed it into every moment and lived experience.

Present-moment awareness transcends all. It breaks the shackles of a meditation session by infusing itself into everything you do.

It's the difference between sitting in meditation and living as meditation. Between intentional practise and effortless presence. Between reacting to life and flowing with it.

Present-moment awareness is the culmination of everything we've explored. Breath, movement, listening, observation, and gratitude, all of it leading to a new way of engaging with the world.

And profoundly, these elements are embodied into the very fabric of our daily lives.

Consider that for a heartbeat.

10

Breaking Out of the Habit Trap

Brace yourself because this chapter is going to take you deep into the mechanics of thought, beneath the very wiring that shapes your perceptions.

It might get more technical than trying to assemble IKEA flat-pack furniture without instructions, but believe me, this information could transform the way you navigate your mind and your life.

But if words like *neocortex* and *subconscious processing* make your eyes glaze over, don't worry, I've slipped a light-hearted bike riding analogy towards the end of the chapter. It summarises all the technical stuff and hopefully makes things a little more digestible.

There's also a raft of practical takeaways, and a condensed checklist summary in the back there too.

So, there's no need to summon your inner neuroscientist unless you want to impress at dinner parties.

What's the bottom line, then?

You get to explore this chapter at your own pace, in your own way. No pressure, no pop quiz, just insight when you're ready for it.

Alright, let's unpack this thing, shall we?

Embracing a new way of life starts with a new way of thinking. And to do that, we must first understand the mechanics of the brain, more specifically the architecture of thought.

Your mind is a vast landscape where the paths you *choose* to direct your thoughts along can lead to enlightenment, trap you in confusion, or land you somewhere in between.

And it is a *choice*; never forget that. You are the constant creator of your own existence through the choices you make, as am I.

Consider this:

It stands to reason that a positive state of mind leads to better choices and more positive outcomes, wouldn't you agree?

And the thoughts *you choose to entertain,* if repeated, embed themselves in your grey matter over time. Is that a fair comment?

With enough repetition eventually, those thoughts become automatic. Can you argue with that?

So, if all that's true, *which it is,* why would anyone *choose* agitation over a positive mindset as a baseline? An endless cycle of agitated thinking simply breeds more of the same.

That's where understanding how a *mindset* evolves becomes essential. More importantly, how do we loosen it up and prepare it for change?

Let's be honest. The human mind isn't exactly a tidy blueprint that's easy to navigate.

We're going to need to simplify, but we must make sure we pull up short of oversimplifying. So, before we go spelunking into the psyche, I want you to know I'll do my very best to keep the twists understandable and relevant, and the metaphors at least *mildly* entertaining.

Alright, take a big, deep breath because it's time to explore your brain somewhat. There's probably a lot of *rewiring* to do, and it might get tricky, so you may want to hold on tight.

No Flies on You

At the heart of it all is a simple relationship between your conscious mind (governed largely by the *neocortex*), and the subconscious mind (run by the deeper systems beneath), where unseen *patterns of behaviour* thrive.

It's in your conscious mind where *deliberate thought* takes place. And to get a real feel for what's coming, we need to unpack that term *deliberate thought*. Let's use the humble fly to illustrate:

Flies are everywhere. Even now, I could glance out the window and spot one. But how often do you actually notice them?

When you *do*, that's *conscious*. When you don't, that's *subconscious*. The flies are still there regardless, right? That's the difference.

Picture this: it's a summer weekend morning and you're milling around in your backyard, barely in second gear.

You sink into a deckchair preparing for your first sip of morning coffee, and a fly lands on your upper lip.

It immediately grabs your attention because it tickles like hell. You swipe at it with your arm, and the fly takes off. Looking for another opportunity to annoy you.

That's conscious: *deliberate thought*. The touch of the fly, the motion of your hand, all being processed in the *neocortex*.

You watch the fly closely as it circles around a few times, then finally comes to rest on your forearm. You're curious, so you *study* it for a few seconds—all of that too, is *deliberate*—therefore *conscious thought*.

It's conscious by virtue of you being *aware of* what's happening in that moment.

Now, back to the scene.

You finish your coffee and decide you better get the chores done before you get yelled at. You ready yourself, pick up the whipper snipper, fire it up, and pull the trigger.

Just as it hits high revs for the first time, the line snaps and your agitation sparks to life.

You stomp to the shed, grab the spare line, stomp back. You grapple with the snipper like you're wrestling a greased pig. You poke about trying to thread the line relying on knee propping to keep it stable.

Today, the *trimmer* is more argumentative than ever (it's never us, right?). The cussing begins, and the agitation escalates.

Eventually you win the war, trim the lawn edges, kill the motor and throw the snipper in the corner of the shed—job done.

And my point? Through that whole whipper snipper ordeal, flies were buzzing, tickling, and landing all around you, while you swatted at them with gay abandon—*that's* subconscious.

Because you were preoccupied; consciously engaged elsewhere, you were oblivious to the flies. And, in all likelihood, the swatting in particular, was being managed by your *subconscious*.

Habits: The Rhythm's Beneath Action

Neuroscience: How Your Brain Wires Reason and Rhyme

Have you ever wondered *why* we sometimes run on autopilot? Why things just happen and what the implications are? Well, neuroscience holds the answers.

Neuroscience is the scientific study of the nervous system, the brain, and the intricate workings of our neural network.

Combined, they govern the complex interplay of thought, emotion, memory, and bodily control that shapes our daily human experience.

The key aspect of the science for you and me here, is how habits form, and how *neural pathways* link cues, routines, and rewards.

We'll get to that in more detail shortly, but first, let's take a high-level look from a technical perspective.

Thoughts or actions begin in the conscious mind. They could be anything: noticing a fly, fretting over the mortgage, or a close call in traffic. Each time we repeat that thought or action, a groove forms in the brain (neuroscience calls it a *neural pathway*).

Over time, those grooves deepen and the more they're repeated, the more established they become (the *neural pathway* is strengthened). Eventually, the subconscious mind no longer needs guidance from the conscious mind, so it takes over running the process.

That's when the behaviour *(process)* becomes automatic *(habit)*. Some habits serve us. Others quietly undo us.

When *neural pathways* become automated, they shape us almost entirely, and nearly always without our conscious awareness.

Are you with me so far? Good, because this is where it gets really interesting.

When a deep-seated *neural pathway* fires, it causes a chain reaction in the body that bypasses the *neocortex*; that part of the brain that lets you know something is going on.

Think about the implications here: when the *neocortex* is bypassed, the fly on the wall, or the tightening in your chest, or the shift in your mood don't register. But they still happen.

The *process* is running in the shadows, without your knowledge or your permission, and herein lies the danger. If we relate that back to our agitated souls. What does it mean? What does it tell us? It means, much of the angst, the restlessness, the frustration, has been quietly engineered *beneath our awareness*.

While we've been busy living, these unseen circuits have been deepening their grooves, shaping our reactions, our moods, even our sense of self—all without our knowledge or consent.

Have I lost you yet? Good, because there's an integral piece of the puzzle we have yet to dissect: *dopamine*.

Dopamine, a *neurotransmitter* central to motivation and reward, plays a pivotal role here. It reinforces habits (good and bad) by linking cues to routines through anticipation and satisfaction.

Deep within the brain, the *basal ganglia* (no need to get hung up on the technical term), act as the silent architect of habit. Here, motivation, reward processing, and the execution of well-worn routines are orchestrated largely outside our conscious awareness.

This network doesn't ask for permission, it simply runs the programs we've rehearsed, whether they serve us or sabotage us.

Alongside its role in motor control and procedural learning, the *basal ganglia* also integrate emotional signals. That makes them a key player in how habits form, stick, and shape our state of mind.

But here's some good news: our brain isn't fixed. It's constantly evolving through a process called *neuroplasticity*. The brain can adapt, reorganise, and rewire itself based on experiences, learning, and environment.

That means existing habits aren't a life sentence. We can reshape them with intentionality, forming new *neural connections* in the process.

Intentional vs Automatic: A Brain in Two Modes.

Let's back over it together, just one more time, to lock it in before we move on.

Every thought and action, deliberate or reflexive, falls into one of two modes: *conscious* or *subconscious*. One requires intention, the other runs on autopilot.

Conscious behaviours are those we actively and intentionally choose with full cognitive awareness. They demand focus and are powered by the *neocortex*, the brain's command centre for intentional thought.

Subconscious behaviours operate beneath the surface via *neural pathways*. They're automatic, instinctual, and shaped by past experiences. Driven by learned patterns, emotions, and internalised beliefs, they influence our actions without our explicit awareness.

They operate on a more intuitive and emotional level, often bypassing the *neocortex* altogether.

Hopefully, you're starting to feel more comfortable with the interplay between the conscious and subconscious, and the relationship they share.

Now, let's take a look at how habits are triggered.

What Triggers Habit Loops?

By now it should be clear: despite the majority of our daily routines being *subconscious*, they aren't random. They follow deeply ingrained *behavioural patterns* shaped by internal drives and external cues.

The more they repeat, the more automated they become.

A *pattern of behaviour* requires conscious input; it's still being shaped, still under construction, therefore seated in conscious thought.

But once that pattern migrates into the *subconscious*, it settles into a deep neural groove in the vault alongside our beliefs and memories, and it begins to run on autopilot. It's now a *habit*: effortless, instinctive, invisible.

Habits don't just run at random; they're attuned to specific signals. Like a well-trained dog waiting for the whistle, they lie dormant until something sets them off.

When a familiar stimulus is sensed, the habit fires. This is where *triggers* (also called *cues*) come in. Think of them as the spark that sets the whole routine in motion.

> Every time we repeat a thought, the groove deepens until behaviour (process) becomes automatic (habit).

Triggers can come from anywhere: from within, such as a fleeting emotion, a stray thought, a physical sensation; or from the outside world, such as a familiar place, a specific person, even the time of day.

They're the quiet hand on the shoulder that says, *"We've been here before; let's run the script."*

The Neocortex: The Role of Your Inner Strategist

Let's dig deeper, because there's a part of the *neocortex* that has the power to call time-out on a runaway habit loop – if you let it.

It's called the *prefrontal cortex*, and it's the seat of planning, prioritising and weighing long-term outcomes. This is where you can pause, consider, and choose.

It's where you can question assumptions, apply logic, and follow rational arguments.

It integrates sensory inputs from the outside world with emotions and memories from within, then uses abstract reasoning to form conclusions and judgements (assuming everything is going to script).

And perhaps most importantly for our purposes, it's adaptable. Cognitive flexibility means you can adjust your choices in response to new information or shifting circumstances.

How Cognitive Processes Influence Habit Control.

When it comes to reshaping habits to shift out of agitation, this adaptability is essential. To put that in context, being mindful of our habits (*patterns* of agitation) and the situations that prompt them (*triggers*) increases our awareness, and awareness gives us control.

Do you see what I'm getting at? It's a *choice*.

I want to revisit something from earlier in the chapter; a question I asked you then, but which should hit differently now:

> *If all that is true—which it is—why would anyone choose an agitated state over a positive mindset as a baseline?*

Reframing the narrative exposes the unseen. We can't stop reacting to triggers if we're not consciously aware they're being stimulated.

And here's the pivot: when you make it *conscious*, you flip the script.

When your response to a trigger is processed *consciously* instead of *subconsciously*, something profound happens. *Conscious processing shapes you by shaping the habit.* Not the other way around.

That's a reversal of power.

You can begin to see the cycle now:

> *Awareness* → *adaptability* → *reflection* → *control.*

When we change how we think, we change what we do. And when we change what we do, we change who we become.

Did I Hear a Penny Drop?

Wait a minute ... so, you're telling me, if I change how I **think**, *I can change ... everything?*

Mindfulness is the key—it's your new superpower!

In this context, it means meta-cognitive reflection: noticing your habits, questioning the thought patterns that drive them, and doing it all *without judgement.*

A pattern of behaviour involves conscious input; a subconscious routine is a habit.

When we respond to a *trigger* consciously, we take the pen back from the subconscious and begin writing the next scene ourselves. We uncover the deeper reasons for our agitated behaviour, the buried scripts, the old grooves.

The task now is to keep those buried scripts in the light where they can be seen, questioned and reshaped.

That kind of emotional awareness goes beyond just insight; it's the first step toward meaningful change.

Why Emotions Cement Habits

When emotion gets added to the mix, our agitated outbursts begin to make a lot more sense. The basal ganglia subconsciously fuses feelings with habit, often before we realise it's happening.

Every habit carries an emotional signature. Joy, stress, frustration – all emotions shape its depth and durability. That's their nature. They leave fingerprints on our habits, shaping how we respond, and what we repeat. It's all part of the game.

Emotions act as powerful anchors, tethering behaviours to pleasure or pain. When intense feelings like love, anxiety, or agitation accompany a habit, the brain floods our system with neurotransmitters, stamping the moment into memory.

That's why we're more likely to repeat a behaviour when similar feelings resurface. These emotional echoes linger longer and hit harder, tightening the bond between trigger and response.

Over time, familiar emotional cues can activate habits before we've had a chance to choose, deepening the groove, and reinforcing the loop.

But with deliberate repetition, we can shift our emotional bias, strengthen positive associations, and loosen the grip of those rooted in distress.

This brings us to the neural crossroads, where habit and intention collide. The dynamic push-pull between the *neocortex* and the *subconscious mind*, the two architects of our behaviour.

This is the seat of choice. *Mindfulness* lifts automatic routines into conscious reach. Now you're back in control, able to use the mechanics of habit formation to your advantage.

The cycle is known as *The Habit Loop*. Understanding it gives us the tools to rewire not just our agitated patterns, but any part of ourselves we're ready to reshape.

The Habit Loop: Trigger (Cue), Routine, Reward

Alright, let's distil this into one clean loop:

At its core, habit formation follows a simple, predictable cycle—trigger (cue), routine, reward.

This loop is the brain's shorthand. It's a streamlined system for efficiency. Once a habit is formed, the brain no longer deliberates; it simply responds. The trigger lights the fuse, the routine runs its course, and the reward seals the deal.

Trigger (Cue):

The spark that sets the habit in motion. Be it an interruption, thought, a time of day, a mood swing, or even the ripple effect of a previous behaviour.

Routine:

The action that follows. The behaviour that fills the gap. It might be a *doomscroll* spiral, a snack raid, or a sunrise jog. The routine is the script your brain runs in response to the trigger.

Reward:

The payoff. A mood shift, a dopamine hit, a sense of control or comfort. Whatever the brain tags as *worth it*, reinforcing the loop and making it more likely to repeat.

Rewards aren't always positive, at least not in the way we'd consciously define them. Some are simply *felt* as positive because the brain floods the system with neurotransmitters (dopamine, most notably) when the routine is triggered.

Have you ever met someone who seems to thrive on emotional friction? The kind who always finds themselves in conflict, chaos, or crisis, not by accident, but by emotional necessity.

For them, the agitation *is* the reward. The drama delivers the dopamine.

It's not that they enjoy suffering, it's that their brain has learned to associate emotional turbulence with a sense of aliveness. And so, the loop continues.

Breaking Down the Habit Loop

Every time we respond to a trigger, we receive a reward: a feeling, a shift, a payoff.

That reward teaches the brain to reinforce the connection, tightening the loop between cue and routine. This is reinforcement learning in action: the brain fine-tunes behaviour based on outcomes, steering us toward comfort, satisfaction, or familiarity.

Most of this happens beneath the surface, outside conscious awareness. But here's the twist; the strength of our *subconscious programming* depends on how often we intervene.

And that's where *mindfulness* enters.

It's the bridge. The moment we pause, notice, and choose differently, we interrupt the loop. We lift the automatic into the conscious.

We take the pen back.

And that brings us full circle (*pun roundly intended*) back to the beginning.

Rewiring the Habit Loop Through Reinforcement

So, here's the essence: habit transformation isn't about battling your agitated soul — it's about rewiring it.

Habits don't define us—we define them.

Over time, emotional biases have shaped your automated responses, embedding themselves through repetition.

We've all been there; the needle won't thread, the toast burns, and suddenly the world feels like it's conspiring against us. These knee-jerk reactions aren't choices. They're rehearsed.

But here's the standout truth: habits don't define us. We define them. That's the difference between living life in default and living life by design.

And with *mindful awareness* as our bridge, we now hold the power to rewrite the loop.

Here endeth the technical stuff ... and not a moment too soon.

Stop the Ride. I Want to Get Off!

Oh, come now, that wasn't so bad. Or was it?

If your brain feels like it's been put through a spin cycle, go grab some painkillers; God knows you've earned it.

If you found it interesting, though, revisit this section from time to time. It really does turbocharge the application of both mindfulness and meditation.

But before your brain starts drafting a resignation letter, let's change the pace. We've been in the weeds of the *operations manual* for a while. Vital stuff, but hardly the kind you frame and hang in the lounge.

Time to step out of the lab and relate it to something a little more human.

From Conscious Effort to Subconscious Mastery

It's really no more complicated than this: your *conscious mind* is like the micromanaging boss; always in meetings, convinced nothing happens without them.

Your *subconscious* is the quiet CEO in the corner office, rubber-stamping the big stuff while the boss fusses over which font to use in the PowerPoint.

But habits form whether you're paying attention or not. The only question is whether you're the one writing them, or they're writing you.

Let's look at it through the lens of learning to ride a bike. It starts with curiosity and a bit of excitement. You see someone gliding effortlessly on two wheels, and think to yourself, *"I want to do that!"*

At first you wobble around a bit, overthink every pedal push, and your conscious brain works overtime. It's a sponge, soaking up every part of the experience: balance, pedalling, steering.

But with repetition, and a few spectacular spills (that add to the thrill), your neurons strengthen their connections.

You're hyper-aware of every muscle movement, every connection, every small win.

Then, at some point, when a sufficient level of skill has been reached, the boss hands the file to the CEO.

Why does this happen? Because the conscious brain has limited capacity. To free up space, it shifts well-rehearsed patterns into the background, where the *subconscious* runs them on autopilot.

From then on, the blueprint is stored and retrieved without conscious involvement. That frees your attention for new challenges and skills you have yet to master.

What was once awkward becomes second nature. Before you know it, you're zipping around without thinking about balance, pedalling, or steering.

And you can apply that methodology to any new learning.

It's the same effect we talked about in the *drive home from work* example from an earlier chapter. That eerie moment you arrive home without remembering the journey.

That's your subconscious running the show while the boss daydreams.

Become the quiet architect of your own mind.

Once you understand the interplay between the boss and the CEO, you realise it's not a lot to remember because the application is universal.

Whether it's riding a bike, driving home, or breaking a bad habit, the same handover happens every time.

We stop being consciously aware and get *preoccupied* with all the noise: the meetings, the emails, the ambitions, the dinner plans.

Yet, those preoccupations don't exist in the now, they're borrowed thoughts dressed up as reality.

That's the end game for most of us. We hand the reins to habit, and the small efficiencies take care of themselves.

But here's the danger: in the quiet shuffle from conscious to automatic, life's richest moments can get swept into the same basket as the menial.

When the treasures are shelved alongside the trivial, the days pass, but the light dims. The moments that once made life vivid fade into the background hum of habit.

Congratulations to us! We've unravelled the mechanics of habit formation.

And well done to you. You've earned this moment, not just for reading it, but for staying curious.

Now, the heavy lifting is done. You've scaled the scaffolding of habit mechanics and survived the spin cycle, a little dizzy, no doubt, but infinitely more equipped to tackle what's next.

Now comes the part where theory meets theatrics, where insight becomes action.

Let's get practical, with a crisp set of habit change strategies, specifically designed to interrupt the groove of automated living.

With practise, you will be able to reshape the loop and get back into the driver's seat.

And once we've laid that foundation, we'll roll into the next chapter, where we layer these strategies with specific mindfulness techniques that make habit change stickier than Mum's famous pecan-and-maple-syrup pie left out on a hot summer windowsill.

Tools for Habit Change

Identify Triggers and Cues: Recognise the *cues* or *triggers* that initiate your unwanted habits. Become more aware of them so you can interrupt the habit loop before it progresses.

Replace Negative Habits with Positive Alternatives: Instead of focussing solely on eliminating a bad habit, replace it with a positive behaviour. For example, if you tend to stress eat, try taking a walk or practising deep breathing instead.

Practise Mindfulness and Self-Awareness: Continue to cultivate your state of mindfulness to observe your thoughts, emotions, and behaviours *without judgement*.

This will help you become more attuned to your habits and make more conscious choices that align with your goals.

Set Specific and Achievable Goals: Establish clear, measurable goals for habit change. Break mountains down into manageable molehills to increase motivation and track progress effectively.

Utilise Positive Reinforcement: Reward yourself for successfully changing a habit.

Positive reinforcement strengthens new neural connections associated with desired behaviour, making it more likely to stick.

Celebrate with intention. Light a candle, sip a ceremonial tea, or mark the moment with a small ritual. Physical acts can signal closure and affirm progress.

Create a Supportive Environment: Surround yourself with people, spaces, and resources that echo the change you're making.

Social support is catalytic. It plays a significant role in sustaining habit change.

Practise Consistency and Persistence: Changing habits takes time, effort, and repetition.

It's crucial for rewiring neural pathways and establishing lasting change. Consistency carves the groove, and persistence keeps it open, especially when setbacks try to close it.

Seek Professional Guidance: Sometimes, a fresh perspective is the missing piece.

A therapist, coach, or wise old sage; someone who speaks your language and sees your blind spots, can offer strategies, accountability, and the kind of motivation that stays with you.

Onward and Upward

By applying these evidence-based strategies informed by neurology and psychology, you can effectively rewire your brain.

Over time, you will cultivate healthier behaviours that align with the values and aspirations that help you break free.

Here's your quick-grab guide for the road ahead:

- **Notice the cue** before it fires.
- **Swap the groove** for something gentler.
- **Use mindfulness** as your spotlight and mirror.
- **Set goals** that fit your feet.
- **Celebrate small wins** and sculpt big shifts.
- **Build a tribe** that cheers the version of you you're becoming.
- **Repeat. Persist. Rewire…and…**
- **If you need a guide**, find one who speaks your language.

Perspective matters.

See these as invitations, not as chores, and use them to turn knowledge into a new rhythm. Think of your agitated soul, not as a problem, but a signal to dance differently.

Kudos to you, once more; you're becoming the quiet architecture of your own life-change.

If your brain feels a little stretched, good. That means you've grown. So take a breath and let the dust settle. You've earned the pause, and the right of passage. Because what comes next turns what you have just absorbed into illumination.

In the next chapter, we're going to layer these strategies with the kind of mindful attention that turns habit change from effort into art.

You've built the stage. Now let's light it up.

The Calm Amidst the Chaos

11

The Science of Sticky

This world is teeming with catchphrases which, like anything that gets overused, can dilute their potency.

This one never loses its truth: *habits are hard to break*.

Most people would stop at habit change and wonder why they struggle to make meaningful progress. They learn the mechanics, pick a few strategies, and call it a day.

And sure, that's progress. But it's like building a beautiful house and never wiring it for electricity. The structure is there, but it's dark inside.

What we're doing here is different, deliberately so.

We're not settling for a single-layer approach. We're building on the habit change premise we set up in the last chapter, broadening its reach and depth by fusing it with specific, practical, and highly targeted mindfulness techniques.

It's a double-whammy because it not only focusses on the change but also builds your mindfulness muscles along the way.

It's the difference between pushing a boulder uphill and having the ground itself rise to meet you. More importantly, these practices aren't standalone hacks. They're amplifiers.

They infuse your habit work with attention, compassion, and emotional clarity. They make the changes you've worked so hard to set in motion, less like a battle and more like a partnership.

When you combine habit change strategies with mindfulness, you don't just change what you do, you change how you see *everything*.

Mindfulness Tools for Habit Change

Here are some essential mindfulness practices paired with each habit change exercise to help form empowering habits and gently dissolve harmful ones:

Identify Triggers and Cues

To spot the cue before it fires, practise ***Mindful Awareness***. Presence with your thoughts, emotions, and actions reveals the subtle sparks that initiate your loops. The more you notice, the more you can *choose*.

Replace Negative Habits with Positive Alternatives

Urge Surfing helps you ride the wave of discomfort without reacting.

This is how it works: in those moments when cravings inevitably arise, take a deliberate breath and truly observe. Surf the emotional wave instead of being swallowed by it.

This pause creates space to swap the groove for something gentler.

Practise Mindfulness and Self-Awareness

Mindful Journaling turns experience into insight. Document your triggers, triumphs, and emotional echoes.

Language clarifies intention, even with yourself, and reflection reinforces growth.

Set Specific and Achievable Goals

Before setting goals, try a *Body Scan Meditation*. Tune into your physical and emotional readiness. Emotional arcs often harbour in the body, manifesting physiologically and revealing tell-tale signs of intuitive discomfort.

Then set goals that fit your feet; they're easier to walk around in, and far more likely to carry you where you want to go.

Utilise Positive Reinforcement

Loving-Kindness Meditation infuses habit change with warmth. Celebrate small wins with compassion.

Kindness isn't soft—it's strategic.

It rewires the way you relate to yourself, turning progress into fuel instead of pressure. The more you practise it, the more your habits grow in the soil of encouragement rather than fear.

Create a Supportive Environment

Mindful Listening strengthens connection, deepens understanding, and affirms the worth of the person before you. When you're truly present with others, your attention becomes a form of support. It's a subtle signal that says, *I'm here with you.*

Over time, those moments of presence weave into trust, and the tribe you build begins to echo the change you seek, amplifying it in ways you could never manage alone.

Practise Consistency and Persistence

Mindful Breathing anchors you in the now. When setbacks arise, return to the breath. It steadies the mind, keeps the groove open, and reminds you that progress is a rhythm, not a race.

Each inhale is a reset; each exhale, a quiet recommitment to the path you've chosen.

Seek Professional Guidance

The *S.T.O.P. Method* offers a pocket-sized ritual of reset. Stop, take a breath, observe, and proceed with intention.

It's a way to pause before reaching out, and to choose your guide with clarity, not from panic.

The right counsel, sought at the right moment, can turn a stumbling block into a stepping stone.

Get Sticky With It

It's one thing to read about habit change and mindfulness in the comfort of a book. It's another thing entirely to apply them when your phone is buzzing, your coffee's gone cold, and your patience is wearing thin.

That's where the magic happens. Not in sterile laboratory conditions, but in the messy, ordinary moments where your old grooves usually dominate.

For that reason, we're going to unpack a few real-life examples to point you in the right direction.

Take doomscrolling for example. You know the drill: you open your phone to check one thing, and twenty minutes later you're choking on a thread about a celebrity feud between two people you despise.

This is where Urge Surfing can earn its keep. When you feel the pull, name it, breathe through it.

Watch the wave of temptation rise and fall without letting it drag you out to sea.

And just like that, you've reclaimed your time and your headspace. Surfing the urge brings it into conscious awareness. Now you can act on it by changing your routine.

Or picture your morning routine. If it's a blur of alarms, emails, and half-finished vegemite toast, layer in Mindful Breathing and the whole thing shifts.

Three slow breaths before you even get out of bed. A pause before you open your inbox. It's the difference between starting the day and *arriving* in it.

What if a moment of emotional friction occurs. A sharp word from a colleague, an unexpected bill, your plan that falls apart. Your old groove might react, defend, spiral.

But what would your new groove do?

Maybe Loving-Kindness Meditation? A quiet reminder that you can meet this moment—and yourself—with warmth instead of war.

It doesn't erase the problem, but that's not the point. It changes the way you carry it, which is more than half the battle, right?

These are just a few small, deliberate shifts that, over time, change the texture of your days. And the more you practise them in real life, the stickier they get.

Cattle Prod or Carrot Cake?

I feel the need to get real for moment. Let's table a few things that mindfulness isn't in this context, because it's important we keep a balanced approach to change.

Put simply, mindfulness isn't a magic wand you wave over your habits to make them behave. If that's the impression you're starting to form, let's nip it in the bud now.

It's not a self-improvement cattle prod, and it's not a competition to see who can sit the stillest looking most serene.

That's one of the biggest traps; treating mindfulness like a fix.

It's not a fix. It's a friendship. And like any friendship worth having, it requires time, attention, and the occasional awkward silence if that's what it takes.

And while we're busting myths, here's one more: mindfulness doesn't mean you'll never slip up again. You will. We all do.

While it's not helpful thinking that way, acknowledging what *will change* is therapeutic. With mindfulness in your corner, a slip doesn't have to turn into a slide.

You start noticing things sooner, you meet them with a raised eyebrow instead of a raised fist, and you get back on track without the drama.

But once again, it's going to take time.

"Yes, I hear you, we've been here, you said that already."

Yes, I did. And I'll probably say it again, because it's possible your expectations need a gentle hosing down. When the chance comes to remind you, I'm going to take it—with love.

While I'm on my soapbox about what mindfulness isn't, here's a sneaky little one that can be downright destructive—using mindfulness to avoid feeling things.

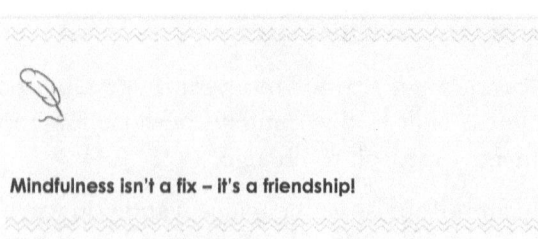

Mindfulness isn't a fix – it's a friendship!

That couldn't be further away from mindfulness.

That's emotional bubble-wrap that muffles life's edges. The point isn't to numb out; it's to notice what's there, even if it's prickly, and to hold it with the same care you would a fragile keepsake.

Life Through the Lens of Sticky Mindfulness

Our agitated souls have caused us plenty of grief over the years, but that doesn't mean we should return the favour. They won't respond well if we go after them with the stick and not the carrot cake. Like any soul, they flinch when mistreated, and flourish when nurtured.

So be gentle with yourself.

You're not here to win gold in the *Mindfulness Olympics*. You're here to weave awareness into the fabric of your days, so that *over time*, the stitches hold fast, even when life tugs hard at the seams.

Big change is built on small, steady moments. The trick is to allow those moments to take root in the soil of your soul, so you don't have to think about *doing mindfulness*, you simply *live* it.

Isn't that the essence of habit formation? When the practice becomes part of you, not something you must remember to do.

Imagine the shift in your life when your *habits* are seated in mindfulness, quietly steering your days from the inside out. And we're only just getting started, so adopting any method that will fast-track the transition is worth considering.

Try these:

Morning Check-In – Before you open your eyes each morning (yes, even before you reach for your phone on the side table), take three slow, deliberate breaths. Notice the air, the rise and fall, the way your body feels.

Then, open your eyes and take in your surroundings as if you're seeing them for the first time. *Maybe you are?* Can you even recall the colour of your bedroom ceiling?

Then, place your feet on the floor and feel them become grounded, at one with it. What does the texture feel like under your toes?

Before the day starts pulling at you, make the time to greet it, to acknowledge that you exist *within* it like a pelican cuddled and carried away on a spring thermal.

Evening Journaling Prompt – Even one line is enough. What loop did I notice today? How did I meet it, and how did I interact with it? Some days you'll write with substance, other days it'll feel more like scribbles in the dark, but they both count.

The point is to keep showing up, because each entry is a thread in a bigger weave.

Over time, these small lines knit together into a living map. One that shows not just where you've been, but how far you've travelled.

Weekly Reflection Ritual – Pick a quiet moment each week to look back. Where did you spot a cue? Where did you swap a groove? Where did you meet yourself with kindness?

It's not about grading yourself; it's noticing the arc of change and the quiet confidence that comes with it.

Okay, let's wrap this up.

Try not to treat any of the practical suggestions in this book as homework. Use them as handrails to keep you steady when life gets slippery.

Let them remind you that change isn't a single leap. Just like learning to dance, it's a rhythm you learn to tango with.

Here's your *Science of Sticky* quick-grab guide:

- **Spot the cue** with Practise Mindful Awareness
- **Swap the groove** using Urge Surfing

- **Observe yourself clearly** by keeping a Mindful Journal
- **Set goals that fit your feet** but do a Body Scan first
- **Celebrate small wins** with Loving-Kindness Meditation
- **Build your tribe** and Listen Mindfully
- **Stay the course** and anchor with Mindful Breathing
- **Seek wise counsel** after pausing with the S.T.O.P. Method

Don't let these *wither on the vine*. Print them out, stick them on your fridge, or tuck them in your wallet so they're there when you need them most.

Better still, pair them with the quick-grab guide from the previous chapter to strengthen the link between them.

You'll also find these, along with all the other practical tools throughout the book, in your *Calm Companions Field Guide* at the back of this book, or downloadable from the website.

From Agitation to Architect

With practice, your *habits* stop bossing you around.

They start working for you, not against you because they become tools instead of traits. Levers you can pull, not chains you have to drag.

Understanding what pokes your agitation only gets us in the game; the game is won by *choosing, with intention*, what you're going to do about it.

That's how you become the quiet architect of your own mind, shaping the blueprint one choice, one breath, one moment of awareness at a time.

Mindfulness *is the light* that shines on your subconscious, so conscious thought can keep it accountable. Habits will still run—that's what they do—but now you're keeping score, and you're calling the shots.

And this is where things shift: armed with steady, deliberate mindfulness at your side, you go beyond managing habits; you transform them.

Eventually, they work out who's in charge and that goes beyond sticky; it's unshakable.

12

Navigating Life's Curveballs

Life can be overwhelming; I know, I've lived it. Some days feel like being trapped in a bounce house full of sugar-laden upstarts in clown wigs and Velcro socks.

And yet, buried somewhere inside the fracas, there's always a crack in the noise longing to be found. A place to grow, a moment to *toughen up*, a chance for positive change.

Ironically, it's not all uphill. Sometimes it's as straightforward as separating the wheat from the chaff, clearing space in your head so you can see what actually matters.

That's where we start: with two glaring dysfunctions of the agitated soul.

One: we keep *choosing* to be pissed at life's curveballs. And two: we treat everything as a curveball.

C'mon ... really. Are we really that self-absorbed we think the world should hit pause while we stew in our own frustrated little tantrums?

I can only speak for myself here, and frankly, that's all I'm doing. But if you're sitting there cowering behind this book with that sheepish, *'busted'* look, it's time to straighten your spine.

And there's a good reason: the bear is about to be poked. It's bound to sting a bit, but that bitter jab of lament pales into insignificance next to the awakening that follows.

We'll get to that later but trust me … it changed everything.

First, let's dive headlong into dysfunction number one: *choosing agitation over rationality*.

Here's the rub: it's not the curveballs, but our reaction to them that matters most. Why duck, if you can knock it out of the park?

Think about it. Just as we have the power to reshape habits, we can rewire the way we meet our triggers.

That's more than philosophy, that's boots-on-the-ground reality. *Choice* ignites change and it shapes who we become far more than the guts, the glory, or the potholes along the way.

But here's the truth, for you, and for me both. Dominion over change has always been ours. Which means, all we have to do is *choose* a different response.

Simple, right? *(he says, wiping the sarcasm from his chin with a figurative tissue)*. But beneath the humour, it's worth letting that truth sink in. It even echoes good old Descartes' famous assertion: *"I think, therefore I am"*.

For me, the real takeaway isn't the Latin, or the philosophy. It's the question it leaves hanging: what if the trigger matters less than the *choice* we make after it fires?

As for the second dysfunction, why is life one big curveball for us? Curveballs only exist because we allow them—*again, by choice*.

Let's not forget, our agitated souls are seasoned professionals, feeding on habits *instigated by us*, and worn smooth by years of over abuse.

Speaking of feeding, they're also a lot like puppies: they'll eat gravel if you feed it to them. So instead of serving up the same emotional diet, maybe it's time to switch up the menu.

Curveball: To Be or Not to Be

What is a curveball anyway? How is one defined?

Life's curveballs are like surprise plot twists in your personal screenplay. Those unexpected challenges that pop up out of nowhere and make you mutter, *"Well, that wasn't in the script!"*

They're like gifts wrapped in gaffer tape: unexpected, frustratingly difficult to unwrap, and rarely what you asked for.

But in the context of this book, we'll keep it simple yet relevant. Let's define a *curveball* as anything that stirs your agitated soul.

If we examine a curveball's trigger *without judgement*, we can make immediate gains simply by thinning the herd. *Choose* what truly deserves the title of *'curveball'* and what should be relegated as background static.

It's a win-win: suddenly not everything's a curveball anymore, and we're sharpening our acumen for *choice*.

Spotting the harmless triggers is now key. Once you name it, you can choose *without judgement* whether it deserves your energy, or you let it slide on by.

If we don't filter by conscious choice, our seasoned agitated souls will pounce on anything, no matter how tiny the spark.

Let's look at some practical examples.

Here's an easy one to get you going: your wireless keyboard dies the second you hit your stride. Sounds petty, right? But stay with me. Pause for a second and notice how it actually makes you *feel*.

What if your coffee lid doesn't seal and dribbles down your wrist, or the paper runs out with one more page to print?

Or how about the sticky note that refuses to cling to your monitor? Or the tissue box that lets the next tissue fall back into the abyss the moment you pull one out?

I could do this all day.

Are these curveballs? Well, it depends on who you ask. But try telling an agitated soul they're not, and watch the sparks fly.

Truth is that these tiny fracases used to send me into a spiral.

Right now, you're either nodding in ashamed solidarity, or silently thanking the universe you're not me—and suddenly feeling much better about yourself.

But hey, at least one of us is getting perspective.

These examples show just how unkind life can be for an agitated soul. What kind of existence is it when your critical deadline derails because a tissue fell back inside the box?

Curveballs only exist because we allow them to —through choice.

If you think I need therapy, meet the *King of Agitatia* – my dear old dad. God bless his cotton socks. I've seen him lose it over things so absurd they make my *episodes* look like light warm-ups.

And I try not to judge. Partly because I've got no right, but mostly because I haven't walked in his shoes. I don't know the torment he's endured, or more to the point, he's put himself through. Let that one settle.

As for me, I've lost count of how many *episodes* where, in the brutal post-mortem, I was unable to name the trigger.

Were they all really that trivial? Or was I was so consumed by the agitation itself that I couldn't recall what sparked them?

Sometimes it's felt like living in agitation *ad infinitum*.

That's why we must go for the low-hanging fruit first. Cull the weak triggers from the herd and practise letting them go.

The answer really is that simple—no matter how difficult it is to do.

Break in the Clouds ... or the Eye in the Storm

We now have a simple place to begin. Remember, all good things take time, so be patient. Start with the incidents you feel you can actually handle.

When the next tissue falls back inside the box, don't just cuss and tear at the box. Sit with it for a few seconds. Notice how it lands in your body: the mental twitch, the slight tightening behind the ribs.

Ask yourself why. Keep unpacking until you can name the trigger, then observe it for a beat, and release it. Repeat the process whenever other triggers arise and celebrate small victories along the way.

It slowly becomes part of your rhythm, quietly shaping the way you meet each day, and then, one day, a single moment will stand out—the one you'll look back on as *defining*.

At least that's how it happened for me. Let me walk you through it, step-by-step.

The spark was one of my repeat offenders—the ill-fitting compost bin liner. *(Yes, I said bin liner. Please, don't judge me ... yet.)*

I remember it like it was yesterday: I was standing in my kitchen, compost bin liner in hand.

The ridiculous scene that followed cracked the shell I'd been living in. It was the first time I can remember thinking, *"this is real – it's actually happening"*.

The Setup: The compost bin is full. I remove the bursting liner, tie it off, dispose of it, then reach for a new one.

I blow into the bag to open it up, drop it into the benchtop bin, lift the handle on one side and stretch the liner over the edge, then set the handle down to lock it in place.

So far so good.

The Trigger: I lift the second handle, stretch the liner, push the handle down to lock it in place, and *rip* – the first edge pops free. Instantly, I'm predator still and steely-eyed, like a maniacal bull sizing up a matador.

The Eruption: My body doesn't flinch, but my mind's already at a rolling boil. A few contemptuous bull-like snorts later, I dive back in.

I reseat the first side, lock it … and the second one dislodges.

The Fallout: Fragments of compost bin go flying across the kitchen and now I have to jump online to order a replacement.

The Analysis: This is not a comedy sketch, my friend.

This was a genuine and frequent trigger. The kind that used to rattle the cage of my agitated soul at the drop of a hat. And it was beginning to alarm me, which is why I had to change.

How did things get so bad?

Maybe the bin liner *episode* was the straw that broke the camel's back. The moment when all the worldly pressures, hidden triggers, and everyday burdens I'd been carrying finally boiled over.

Or maybe it was my incessant pursuit of perfection. I used to fling the battle cry *"Why can't they just make shit that works?"* with alarming regularity.

Whatever the reason, things were real now. *Conscious thought* had finally superseded *subconscious routine*.

The Solution: Lean in for this one because I'd hate for you to miss any of the magic.

Everything shifted the instant I accepted *what is,* instead of clinging to what *Agitated Soul* demanded. It was the toughest truth to swallow, yet also the most unexpectedly liberating; like breathing clean air after years underground.

Up until then, my authentic self had been buried under the years of rubble from old, agitated habits, hair-trigger reactions, and the history I kept hauling around.

But that day, it broke through, and *Agitated Soul* did not appreciate being challenged.

I sat in the moment, still fuming, neck-deep in a cesspool of the fury, and yet, through the steam, I was able to *observe* the trigger.

I finally *saw* the absurdity of living life as an agitated soul. I could label the compost bin liner *episode* for what it was: a triviality.

Most importantly, the trigger was uncoupled from the circumstance. I could watch it drift away on its own current, and in that moment, the agitation dissolved like the outer layer of chocolate on a Mars Bar baking in the hot summer sun.

That was the moment the ground shifted beneath my feet—the irreversible turning point.

And here's the gold-embossed silver lining. The very next episode—not six months later, not twenty episodes later—the very next one, was unrecognisably different.

The fury fizzled like a rogue firecracker instead of roaring like a bushfire, and the clarity cut through at a blistering pace by comparison.

Even under pressure, the act of observing the trigger was sharper, truer, and far more vivid than I'd ever felt before.

Triviality: Get in the Back Seat – And Stay There

I can't overstate how game-changing it is when you *straighten your spine* and really see what's going on. The sooner you start, the sooner things shift.

You'll still have a long way to climb, but the first huge leap off the pit floor can feel almost instantaneous.

When your next *episode* looms, first check in with yourself. Can you handle the oncoming charge?

Our agitated souls are ferocious SOB's, and there's no shame in stepping back if you're not ready. Even then, you're a step closer to freedom, because the agitation is still *conscious*.

So, pick your battles and ease into it. When you do take it on, sit with it for as long as you can. At first it might feel like lowering yourself into a bath that's a shade too hot, but hold steady. When the temperature settles, go to work—methodically.

Observe the trigger. Break it down. Ask: *"is this a genuine tribulation or just a trivial irritant?"* If it's trivial, keep observing. What exactly about it has you so riled up?

The longer you hold it in your sights, the clearer it becomes. When you begin to see how much of your life has been hijacked by this relentless, automated agitation, that's the moment your agitated soul doesn't stand a chance.

If I have the power to allow myself to become an agitated soul, then I have the power to rise above it.

Don't stall, even if the speed of change feels glacial. Progress is a delicate dance with one foot in comfort, the other in challenge.

Set small, winnable goals, and actually celebrate them. But keep the weight of change light enough to carry.

Eventually, control comes back to you. You'll start recognising how many triggers are pure triviality, and that's when the seismic shift happens.

Look back at my own examples. As silly as they sound, they were real spark-points for me. The wake-up call was seeing the absurdity. Sure, I have genuine struggles, ones that would concern most.

And herein lies the crux: feed your agitation with petty frustrations, and when real struggles arrive, they'll grow into battles bigger than they ever needed to be. Sometimes, bigger than you can handle.

Sting Like a Bee

I think it's prudent to pause and reflect on the transition from agitation to awareness one more time.

Agitation doesn't announce itself. It creeps in quietly, blending the trivial with the turbulent until you're knee-deep in frustration, unsure how you got there.

The tricky part is that it plays out beneath the surface; a cycle of automated reactions firing before *conscious thought* even gets a chance to step in.

Being *mindful* of the trivial doesn't mean genuine tribulations won't still enter the fray. You and I carry emotional strain many couldn't fathom, so we need to be pragmatic about this shift.

It's not easy to dismiss the trivial when tribulation is present. For us, they don't separate; they compound.

That's why it's critical we learn how to carve out the difference.

And here's a comforting thought: the universe didn't single us out for special torment. Everyone's dodging curveballs, even that annoyingly cheerful neighbour who looks like they've got life all neatly gift-wrapped.

Still, I hear you. Some days, it *does* feel like the universe is running a personal vendetta of biblical proportions.

But *perspective* can move mountains.

Separate the wheat from the chaff and you start to see life through a different lens. That's when healing begins.

The moment we realise we have more control than we give ourselves credit for, and we lace that control with a little self-compassion, the road ahead suddenly feels far less rocky.

React swiftly to trivial triggers, acknowledge them, then stamp them out by watching them drift away. Shake things up. Start rewiring that brain of yours.

Life is one giant obstacle course. Be comfortable with the fact that some days, you'll sidestep gracefully, others, you'll wipe out spectacularly.

So, step into the ring like a prize-fighter and float like a butterfly for a while. Eventually, you'll be stinging like a bee.

Now, before we get too pleased with ourselves, we should address the elephant in the room.

Has the Buck Stopped Yet?

How did we become agitated souls in the first place?

And, more importantly, who's to blame? If I'm honest, the trail leads somewhere uncomfortably close to home.

Why? Because of the decisions we made while stumbling through life, learning how to cope without a net.

Confession time:

I could have stopped the *agitational build-up* simply by *choosing* to respond differently to life's little challenges from the get-go.

But I didn't. I let it slip, almost unnoticed, into the *subconscious*. Over decades, it festered and took me over. I'm tipping the same might be true for you.

At the risk of overstating it, I want to make sure my sentiment is crystal clear here. I'm not sharing this declaration in hindsight, I'm confessing it to you *right now*, in real time, as I write.

It's a profound awakening so raw ... it almost hurts to share. But what kind of author would I be if I cherry-picked my vulnerabilities?

Owning up to that feels strangely freeing. Like shedding a load, I didn't even realise I was carrying. Try it sometime, it's positively cathartic.

> **React swiftly to trivial triggers, acknowledge them, then stamp them out by watching them drift away.**

Vulnerability has a way of embracing you like nothing else can. Of making you feel human, right to the bone, doesn't it?

Sure, it's easy to say that now, but in the thick of agitation, it's another story altogether. Still, it's the truth.

"I am the master of my fate; I am the captain of my soul!"

And so are you.

Those lines close William Ernest Henley's 1875 poem, *Invictus;* a testament to resilience and accountability.

They've vibrated in me for years, a reminder of both the burden and the power of self-determination.

I want to share the poem with you here:

INVICTUS by William Ernest Henley

Out of the night that covers me,
Black as the pit from pole to pole,
I thank whatever gods may be
For my unconquerable soul.

In the fell clutch of circumstance
I have not winced nor cried aloud.
Under the bludgeonings of chance
My head is bloody, but unbowed.

Beyond this place of wrath and tears
Looms but the Horror of the shade,
And yet the menace of the years
Finds and shall find me unafraid.

It matters not how strait the gate,
How charged with punishments the scroll,
I am the master of my fate,
I am the captain of my soul.

I was captivated by those last two lines the moment I heard them. They're a constant reminder that who I've become is of my own making, and sometimes that's very tough to declare.

Now, here I am, well on the road to recovery from '*AA*' (*Agitation Addiction*), thanks in no small part to two lines penned 150 years ago.

They've sat in my mind like a compass, pulling me true when I've been most adrift. Sobering, isn't it?

The Straw That Unbroke the Camel's Back

Time for some good news: if I'm responsible for who I have become, I'm also responsible for who I am becoming. Therefore, if I had the power to let myself become an agitated soul, then I have the power to rise above it.

If that doesn't light a spark—make you want to stand tall and take charge—I'm not sure what will.

See challenges as fuel. Let setbacks be lessons that refine your character and steel your resolve. Learn from the wisdom they offer. Challenges aren't here to break us; they're here to shape us.

Okay, time to throw on your superhero cape, because we're about to deepen our confrontation with the elephant in the room.

The harshest truth. The most jagged of pills.

Facing home truths isn't easy, but it's essential. If a single straw can break a camel's back (*or is it an elephant's back*) then surely removing one can begin to heal it.

Let's start unpacking those straws together, one by one.

The Calm Amidst the Chaos

13

Overcoming Your Biggest Obstacle

Permit me, if I may, to cut straight to the chase. We danced with the elephant in the room last chapter; this time, we're stepping into the ring with it. So, here it is—gloves off.

Most of your obstacles boil down to a single word: you.

That's right, you heard me loud and clear: they come from you. The toughest battles aren't out there; they're the ones you fight in your head.

Don't worry; I'm in this with you. That's why it feels so damn important to haul this one into the light.

We agitated souls get so tangled in self-imposed, subconscious rites and rituals, we sometimes lose track of what day it even is.

It's time to face those limits with strategies that work *with* your emotional wiring, not against it, so your growth feels sustainable, aligned, and anchored in who you are.

Whether it's fear, doubt, procrastination, or any other weakness whispering in your ear, imagine what might unfold if you sidestepped those mental saboteurs with integrity.

Every moment you spend wrestling with your doubts is stealing from your potential. So, shrug off that self-doubt like an overstuffed coat in summer and step boldly forward.

After all, the only thing between you and what you want most ... is *you*. Strip away the hesitation, step forward, and give your future-self something to thank you for.

Remember that mantra—the lighthouse in my storm—I once scrawled in bold, unwavering letters:

> *If you refuse to change, you choose to accept.*

That's the heart of it. What do those words mean to you, now you've come this far?

If it's not yet clear, let me spell it out for you.

Change isn't just about knowing, it's *about choosing*.

You can devour every self-help book, and binge-watch every guru, but unless you stop clinging to old patterns, you'll never break free from your agitated soul.

So, let's sharpen your decision-making instincts with nine *wake-up calls* you can start using *right now* to rewire your agitated soul, and leap tall obstacles in a single bound.

Wake-Up Call #1: *Separate Triviality from Tribulation.*

Not every setback is a catastrophe. We touched on this the previous chapter, but it bears repeating, especially when life's small bumps are masquerading as mountains in your mind. Distinguish between minor nuisances and genuine challenges.

Throwing the toys out of the cot because a sticky note won't stick isn't a curveball; it's a hiccup. Rewrite the damn note and move on.

One of my favourite sayings is, *"Refuse to be distracted by that which you cannot control."* Well, this is the antithesis of it. Stop letting trivial annoyances feed your agitation.

Fix them. Clear them. Move on.

How many times have you ignored a small issue, only to trip over it again and again? The squeaky hinge. The broken zipper.

Things fester. They build and repeat. And they siphon your emotional bandwidth.

> **The only thing standing between you and everything you want ... is you.**

Here's a classic example. You're in the kitchen when the person you're with asks you nicely if you can cut the tomatoes. In that instant, your mind flicks back to the last time you did it and every small frustration that came with it.

Your shoulders inch up. You grip the cutting knife, smiling just enough to hide the grind of your teeth.

The first slice is a disaster; the skin won't pierce. Your jaw tightens as the tomato's structural integrity buckles under the blade. Now your agitation is kicking the door down.

Does this sound familiar? I can feel the agitation simmering as I'm writing this. But here's the thing. No matter how you slice it (pun sharply intended), this is trivial. No debate. No justification. Just sharpen the damn knife!

The sharpener's right there in the knife block. One small fix, and the agitation vanishes before it even has the chance to bite.

When you learn to separate triviality from tribulation, you conserve your strength for the confrontations that count.

It's ok to have drama in your life—it's part of the journey. But unnecessary drama is dead weight.

Be brutally honest: how many of your *episodes* have been trivial?

Remember the old adage, *pick your battles*. Focus your energy on what genuinely matters. Prioritise the things that bring you joy—or at least don't feed your agitation.

Let go of the little distractions that spoon-feed your agitation. Life gets a whole lot clearer. Your energy flows where it's needed most, into relationships, projects, and experiences that light you up.

I know not every obstacle is trivial. But that's the point, right? Cut the nonsense, clear the clutter, and suddenly life feels lighter, sharper, and a hell of a lot more meaningful.

The next wake-up call invites you to tune in to something deeper: the signals life is sending you, whether you're ready to hear them or not.

Wake-Up Call #2: *Listen to the Universe.*

Life doesn't always shout; sometimes it whispers. When it does, is sends subtle signals nudging us in new directions.

Stay open to these whispers, because that closed door you keep cursing might be guiding you towards something better. Something more aligned, more honest, more necessary than you ever dared to imagine.

How many times have you caught yourself asking, *"Why does this keep happening to me?"* More than you'd like to admit, if you're being completely honest with yourself, I bet.

That mindset does more than reflect frustration, it *reinforces it!*

What you project, you attract.

I won't go full bohemian-guru on you, but let's be real: this isn't just spiritual fluff. The law of attraction has practically become a science, or at least an industry.

But instead of parroting the experts, let me offer a little twist that might help shift your perspective.

Instead of obsessing over what you want to pull into your life, consider what you're already manifesting, consciously or not.

Every thought and feeling sends out a signal. The universe then responds in kind to those signals, which shape our reality in ways we often don't see.

Think about those gut-level feelings. The job that felt right. The relationship that didn't. Your internal compass is part of your attraction power.

But we agitated souls can be stubborn SOB's. We override instincts to get our own way—yes, even if it winds us up.

This is where trusting the universe comes in. Maybe she has other plans for you. What if the thing you're chasing isn't meant for you?

And what if the roadblocks aren't part of some cosmic conspiracy at all? Let that land for a second.

Maybe it's not the universe blocking you. Perhaps it's *you*, refusing to turn, clinging to a path that no longer serves.

Next time you catch yourself cussing under your breath, *"why in God's name does this keep happening to me?",* pause. Consider whether you can live without it.

Try letting go, creating space, and listening to the universe. You might be pleasantly surprised by what rushes in to fill the void.

It's like clearing out a cluttered closet; once you've removed the old clothes you never wear, suddenly there's room for something new, something better, something extraordinary waiting just around the corner.

Think about the relationships, habits, or even beliefs you've held onto long past their expiry date. Change *is* daunting and it always will be—that's its nature—as you are about to find out.

Wake-Up Call #3: *Embrace the Flow of Change.*

Change is the only constant. Like a river adapting to its terrain, be willing to carve new paths rather than fighting the flow, even if the water feels colder than you'd like.

Resisting change breeds frustration. Flowing with it opens fresh perspectives and unexpected opportunities. Like the time a job transfer you dreaded dropped you into a city where you met your closest friends.

Every bend in a river reveals new scenery. Embracing change means releasing what no longer serves you; the outdated role, the toxic friendship, the house that's become more storage unit than home.

Step into the unknown with both feet.

Yes, it's scary, but it's also exhilarating. The real question is: will you cling to the bank or ride the current?

So, what are you waiting for? Leap.

Say goodbye to those *'friends'* and circumstances that linger only because of history. Make space for the people, places, and projects that will propel you forward. One's that energise your spirit and honour who you're becoming.

Just as moving on from one long-term relationship can clear the way for a love that lifts you.

Remember, every great story has its ups and downs. The plot twists keep it alive, surprising you just when you think you know. It's all part of the ride.

Just like that river finding its way, when you trust the current, you might drift into a calling you couldn't have paddled to on purpose.

Wake-Up Call #4: *Find Strength in Vulnerability.*

Acknowledging your emotions isn't weakness; it's self-awareness. It's courage. Even the strongest trees bend with the wind, not from weakness, but from survival instinct.

That flexibility is what makes it resilient.

Allow yourself to *feel*. That's how you grow in ways you never imagined. When we embrace our emotions, we give ourselves breathing space to process, softening the urge to bottle things up.

The next time agitation rears its ugly head, don't suppress it. Sit with it. Allow yourself to breathe and reflect. The quiet space you create is where calm lies dormant, waiting to be discovered.

When you're comfortable sitting with your emotions, think about sharing them. Vulnerability is what connects us and sharing with someone you trust can really lighten the load.

So, reach out for support. It's perfectly okay.

Talk to a friend, a family member, a mentor, or even a therapist. Everyone hits rough patches, and we all need a shoulder every now and then.

You may be surprised how many people are willing to lend an ear or offer advice.

There's strength in vulnerability so, before you brush this off, ask yourself, who have you leaned on lately? Did you let them see the real you?

And just as importantly, who may be in need of your ear right now, without judgement, without fixing, just your presence?

If you're still not convinced vulnerability is strength, watch Brené Brown's TED Talk.

If you haven't seen it yet, do yourself a favour and dedicate some quality time to absorb her message. She delivers a masterclass in courage.

She's a respected voice in the field, but more importantly, she walks her talk. The very act of standing on that stage and baring her soul to the world, as she did, exemplifies the courage and authenticity she advocates for.

Through her words and demeanour, she invites the audience to connect with her on a deeply human level.

Her vulnerability in that moment is a powerful reminder: strength lies in being true to oneself and embracing one's imperfections. Honesty over armour.

So, if you've been bracing against the wind, maybe it's your time to bend with it. The obstacle isn't always the storm, sometimes it's our refusal to move with it.

Wake-Up Call #5: *Transform Obstacles into Opportunities.*

History is full of moments in which adversity fuels greatness. Thomas Edison endured thousands of failed experiments, but he didn't see defeat, he saw stepping stones to success.

Stories of those who've risen from the ashes of struggle are truly inspiring. Take J. K. Rowling. She faced rejection after rejection before finally landing a publisher for Harry Potter.

Each setback only strengthened her resolve, proving that perseverance can lead to monumental achievements.

Success stories aren't limited to literature; they're everywhere, especially in sport.

Michael Jordan was cut from his high school basketball team, but he didn't fold. He used that rejection as fuel to transform himself into one of the greatest athletes of all time.

Russell Wilson's TED Talk offers another powerful lens on resilience. As a professional athlete in both baseball and American football, Wilson shares valuable lessons learned from his journey to the top.

> **Change isn't just about knowing, it's about choice.**

His core message centres on the importance of resilience, hard work, and the power of *'neutral thinking'*—a mindset that helps him stay focussed under pressure.

His talk isn't just about sport. It's about life. It's about maintaining a positive mindset in the face of adversity.

For Wilson, greatness isn't measured by medals or accolades; it's measured by the battles you win within yourself.

And for agitated souls, the grandest battle is freeing yourself from its grip—a quiet, internal, skirmish often invisible to others. The kind of triumph that rewires your patterns, restores your peace, reclaims your power. That's *real* greatness.

These stories prove one truth: our greatest trials forge our deepest strengths.

So next time you hit an obstacle, ask yourself: Is this a roadblock ... or an opportunity waiting to be claimed?

Wake-Up Call #6: *Practise Mindfulness, Gratitude and Compassion.*

We've already explored mindfulness, but its role in overcoming agitation obstacles is too vital to skim past.

Agitation and anxiety thrive when we're stuck replaying old scenes or bracing for imagined futures.

Anchoring yourself in the present through breath, observation, or simple daily rituals, helps keep the chaos in check.

Mindfulness isn't just awareness, it's a shift from what's missing, to what's already here.

Gratitude transforms your outlook, not by ignoring pain, but by widening the lens. Compassion, towards yourself and others, fosters connection, healing and purpose.

Mindfulness, gratitude and compassion are all interlinked in a form of *cosmic remedy* for suffering that doesn't cost you a cent.

Still, practising them isn't always easy. It takes patience to sit with discomfort, and courage to meet your own thoughts without flinching. But learning how to breathe through the storm, rather than trying to escape it, is where the shift begins

Life's curveballs can knock you sideways ... or nudge you toward new horizons. It all depends on how you catch them: with clenched fists or open hands.

Are you a writer? Or just someone trying to make sense of the noise? Try journaling your thoughts.

Journaling is a mirror to your mind; a quiet space that welcomes clarity. It's not about perfect prose, just honest presence. Who knows? Maybe there's a masterpiece within you, or maybe just a little peace. Either way, it's worth showing up to the next page.

Wake-Up Call #7: *Set Boundaries to Protect Your Energy.*

It's vital to recognise your limits and communicate them clearly. Just as a garden thrives when properly tended, your well-being flourishes when you safeguard your time and emotional resources.

Saying *no,* when necessary, allows you to say *yes* more often to what truly matters.

A garden thrives not just because it's watered. Keeping weeds in check is a significant contributor. Protecting your energy means keeping invasive demands in check. Those that drain you rather than nourish you.

Some weeds are disguised as opportunity, others as obligation. But if they choke your roots, they have to go.

Think of boundaries not as walls but as gates. Gates you choose to open or close based on what supports your growth.

They're not about shutting people out, but about letting the right ones in. The ones who honour your time, respect your space, and don't mistake access for entitlement.

There's a lyric I carry with me—one of my all-time favourites—in a song by Aerosmith that echoes this:

> *I kept the right ones out*
> *And let the wrong ones in*
> *Had an angel of mercy*
> *To see me through all my sins*

Consider this: if you wouldn't let someone trample your garden, why let them trample your peace?

When your energy is protected, your presence is intentional. Boundaries are as much generative as they are protective. They make space for what's meant to flourish.

Emotional resilience is built through endurance and cultivated through discernment.

Set your boundaries early. Tend to your garden, dispense with the weeds, and let what matters grow.

Wake-Up Call #8: *Seek Solace in Solitude.*

Amidst the chaos, moments of calm can be profoundly healing. It's the heartbeat of this book; the quiet pulse of respite beneath the noise.

Solitude isn't loneliness, it's a return. An opportunity to reconnect with yourself.

Great thinkers like Thoreau, and visionaries like Steve Jobs, retreated into nature for this very reason. They understood that silence speaks when the world stops shouting.

Carve out time to simply be. No obligations. No distractions. Allow yourself the grace to breathe deeply and reflect.

Being still doesn't mean being passive. Practise active listening in these moments. Allow your inner voice, long drowned out by noise, to be heard.

Imagine sitting by a quiet lake. The gentle lapping of water becomes the soothing soundtrack to your thoughts. The world fades away, and in that sacred stillness, your dreams, fears, and desires rise, unfiltered and unjudged.

If solitude feels daunting, start small. Take a walk in a nearby park or invest one hour, reading in your favourite nook.

Each moment counts as you build this sanctuary within.

Reach beyond fleeting distractions; let nature and *your space* envelop you like a warm embrace. There's wisdom waiting there. A deep, endless reservoir from which answers flow once you learn to listen closely enough.

Wake-Up Call #9: *Believe in Your Resilience.*

Human resilience never ceases to amaze me. Look at how we adapted, endured, and ultimately forged ahead to a new kind of normal after COVID-19.

I should know. I lived through it in the most locked down city in the world. And it pushed me to the brink.

If I'm honest, it still haunts me. Lingering ghosts woven into the darker corners of my mind.

During that time my marriage collapsed, my new business venture was hijacked, and my sanity was cracking. I was one dirty look thrown in my direction from a complete psychotic episode.

But I made it through. And now, here you are reading about it.

The pandemic changed everything. No question. But, as I've said time and again, change can bring growth.

Now, we've learned to navigate this new terrain with creativity, adaptability, and the kind of gritty determination that only emerges when the world is tipped on its ear.

Even the strongest trees bend with the wind.

During the pandemic, we began connecting in innovative ways. Virtual gatherings and socially distanced meetups in local parks skyrocketed.

Businesses pivoted, finding new avenues for success that previously didn't exist.

It was our collective adaptability that shone brightly, and it showed us the way. In many ways, we are now more aware of our needs than ever before.

It's likely you're more resilient than you give yourself credit for. You've already proven it, now it's time to believe it.

Resilience isn't the exclusive domain of the collective, it's also personal. I mean, look at you. You're on a pilgrimage toward something greater as we speak—a better you in a better world.

Trust in your innate ability to overcome. You've navigated hardships before, and I'm sure each experience has strengthened you. Let those memories be proof of your enduring spirit.

Take a leaf from nature's book of resilience (pun greenly intended). The lotus flower blooms from filth—untouched and radiant. The bamboo battles unseen beneath the soil, solidifying its foundation before it soars skyward.

And the Phoenix doesn't just endure, it *erupts* from its ashes, reborn with fire.

When the Ashes Settle...

These wake-up calls transform agitation into empowerment. They draw inspiration from trailblazers who came before us.

Thomas Edison refused to see failure as defeat. When asked about his many unsuccessful attempts to invent the light bulb, he replied:

"I have not failed. I've just found 10,000 ways that won't work."

He also said:

"Many of life's failures are people who did not realise how close they were to success when they gave up."

Nelson Mandela endured 27 years behind bars. He could have emerged bitter, but instead, he walked into history carrying a message of unity, reshaping a nation, dismantling apartheid, and becoming South Africa's first Black president.

There's a moment after a storm, after a breakdown, after a burn, when silence returns and something new begins to stir.

And as these words hit the page, a storm breaks outside my window—how deliciously ironic.

That's what this chapter has been guiding you toward. Not just survival, but emergence. Not just healing, but transformation.

You've faced agitation long enough. You've carried its weight for far too long. Now, you hold the tools to stand in defiance of it. These wake-up calls are an invitation to participate in your own recalibration. To pause. To listen. To choose.

No doubt, agitation will knock again. But next time, you'll answer with grace. With boundaries. With breath. With belief.

It's our choices that define us … and change *is* choice.

To embrace change is to rise resilient.

Choose to be a Phoenix … Rise.

The Calm Amidst the Chaos

14

Finding Your Inner Calm

If self-compassion and self-care are foreign concepts to you, embracing them will probably feel like juggling flaming torches while riding a unicycle uphill ... in a hailstorm.

Yet, while difficult, take it from me, it's a fight worth fighting. The reward will match the struggle, step for step, and then some—every single time.

Typing these words feels strange enough to me, so I can only imagine what's running through your mind as you read them right now.

I mean, who wouldn't want to embrace self-compassion, right? It sounds so simple. That's what I thought too ... until I actually tried it.

When I stepped onto the battlefield of mindfulness and meditation, and put myself through the wringer of self-analysis, I was mortified by just how savage I'd been to myself for so many years. And that was only the *conscious* stuff.

Layer that with a torrent of deeply ingrained *habits* of emotional self-abuse, and there you have it: an agitated soul of the highest order, allergic to self-compassion.

Is that how you feel? Wanting to be more self-compassionate, but too damn amped on agitation to even consider the notion.

Living in a loop of desperately needing self-compassion, yet too flooded with angst to accept it, is a maddening paradox.

What should have felt comforting ended up feeling like trying to wrestle a hot, loud, out-of-control, malfunctioning popcorn machine into becoming a capybara.

Picture it: the metal beast bouncing around the room, spewing streams of buttery-rich, salted chaos in all directions. And somehow, you're meant to morph that into the world's most laid-back creature, lazing in a warm spring, eyes half-closed, letting the current carry it as it nibbles contentedly on river grass.

But that's the game we're stuck playing—turning chaos into calm. Self-compassion will help lighten the load.

Even if you're more averse to self-compassion than I ever was, you must make this change. By now you've seen that beating yourself up for being unhappy is a self-fulfilling prophecy. It's a dead-end, pure and simple.

"I'm annoyed."

"Right then, let me emotionally harangue you a little more and see if that helps."

Keep walking that path and you'll wear your spirit to the bone; choose differently, and the load begins to lift.

Just a dash of self-love is enough to get you started. It might be the first real breath you've taken in years. Even the smallest ember can ignite real change.

The good news is the second step towards anything is always easier than the first.

So if you're feeling like a rapscallion popcorn machine in a capybara's world, don't worry, you're not alone.

I've got your back!

Shall we forge ahead and see how we can sift through the chaos? Let's find some kindness for the one who's been waiting for it all along—*you*.

Are You a Teddy Bear or a Grizzly Bear?

I hate to keep saying it, but a transformation won't happen quickly. That's why we hunt for the *moments* of calm amidst our chaos, no matter how fleeting.

Still, the end goal is transformation, is it not?

So which emotional archetype fits you best? The teddy bear approach is gentle, nurturing, and maintenance focussed. Small acts of care that keep the soul humming.

The grizzly bear approach is bold, proud, transformative—the *rip-the-band-aid-off* method.

If your idea of transformation resembles a slow rebuild of a quirky, classic old car, lovingly restored piece by piece, then you're probably the teddy bear type.

Picture a 1969 XW Ford Falcon with plenty of mileage, and even more personality.

Rebuilding takes years of patience, truckloads of care, and the ability to love it as it is, every step of the way.

If you're the *grizzly* type, you'll want to dive headfirst into self-compassion. Complete the transformation fast, scars proudly on show, no apologies. And when you come out the other side, those scars will take on a whole new meaning.

The Japanese art of kintsugi repairs broken pottery with golden lacquer. Instead of hiding the cracks, it celebrates them, transforming the once-shattered item into a unique masterpiece.

Let your battle scars be your armour. Kintsugi teaches us imperfections and struggles aren't flaws to hide away; they're part of our story.

Comedians are brilliant at this. Maybe that's your jam.

> Let your battle scars become your armour.

Here's another angle.

Think of your mind as a cluttered garage, filled with forgotten relics, random junk, and the occasional treasure.

Self-care means clearing out the cobwebs, organising the chaos, and making space for calm to breathe. It's about making room for that hidden gem; that moment of inner peace.

As decluttering icon Marie Kondo might put it, '*Kondo-ing*' your mental space is keeping what sparks joy and discarding the rest.

The garage may never be pristine, but it becomes a space you can navigate with ease, minus the dust-induced sneezes and existential clutter.

Don't Shoot the Messenger

Whichever *bear* you are—teddy or grizzly—your path to inner peace begins with one essential fact: be relentlessly kind to yourself. And if you've been pickled in agitation your whole life, that's easier said than done. I get it.

That constant hum of tension wears you down until it feels like there's no one left to blame. Life begins to resemble a burnt steak: small, tough and with the chips stacked against it.

Self-blame becomes the only option left on the shelf.

But that's not the solution. That's the trap. When you turn on yourself, you're not solving a problem, you're fanning the flames of an already intense inferno.

Bob Ross, the beloved American painter with the soothing voice and the majestic afro, once said: *"We don't make mistakes, just happy little accidents."*

That's not just a philosophy for painting; it's a philosophy for living. Self-compassion means seeing your slip-ups not as failures, but as brushstrokes in a masterpiece still in progress.

So, here's the setup: your canvas is your life, your palette is filled with vibrant self-care practices, and your paintbrush is every choice you make.

Each brushstroke, bold or tentative, adds to the bigger picture. And that picture is you. A one-of-a-kind work of art. Messy in places, radiant in others, but undeniably you.

So go ahead, paint yourself a masterpiece of inner peace. It's been waiting on the inside all along. You just have to let it out.

Peace-ing it all Together

Each analogy we've explored—restoring classic cars, embracing kintsugi, decluttering garages, and painting masterpieces—illuminates a different face of self-compassion:

- Restoration speaks to patience.
- Kintsugi to resilience.
- Garages to mental clarity.
- Painting to self-expression.

Whichever combination resonates with you, the heart of the message remains the same: Transformation requires tending to yourself with patience, care, and forgiveness.

Let's not forget that last one: forgiveness.

Give yourself permission to slip up, to be gloriously, unapologetically human. Let the tiniest sprinkle of chaos bring depth to the beautiful mix of courage and grace.

I know, it's hard. You're wired to push forward, to *get the job done*, to tick the box. That drive makes the process of healing feel uncomfortable by default, and maybe that's exactly the point.

Healing isn't about comfort; it's about courage. It's leaning into discomfort and staying there long enough to grow.

In the long run, inner peace flourishes when you adopt a balanced approach to your journey. Knowing when to hold yourself accountable … and when to let something slide.

Nobody thrives under a tyrant, so don't be one to yourself. Be the compassionate king of your own kingdom.

As you cut through the chaos remember, self-compassion and self-care aren't one-time tasks. They're disciplines, like training for a marathon.

Some days, you'll cross the finish line with arms raised, other days you'll slog through the mud, shoes heavy and spirits low. The key is to keep moving, celebrate small wins, and show yourself favour through the rough patches.

Say 'no' to what drains you and 'yes' to what nourishes you.

And now, in keeping with the theme, here are nine key insights to help you cultivate inner peace. Some may echo earlier ideas, but don't let that fool you—their strength lies not only in the words themselves, but how you live them.

The same principle, applied with fresh awareness, can spark entirely new outcomes.

Mindfulness and Meditation: As with all previous practical applications, this is the foundation, the soil from which everything else grows. It's emphasised throughout the book for good reason.

Start with the simple exercises from earlier chapters. Even a few minutes a day nurture a sense of inner peace.

Think of it as giving your mind a warm, gentle bath, rinsing away the day's noise to make room for calm.

It's like learning to sit by the shore, watching the waves roll in. At first, you might instinctively dive into the turbulence, trying to fight or fix each surge.

But over time, you simply observe. Each wave rises and falls, and you remain steady, no longer pulled under because you're anchored in awareness.

Practise self-compassion: Be kind to yourself. Treat yourself with the same warmth and understanding you'd offer a dear friend in need.

The way you speak to yourself matters, because your inner dialogue shapes your emotional landscape and colours how you see the world.

Self-compassion bridges the gap between self-criticism and self-acceptance, helping you recognise your worth even in moments of fear and doubt.

Imagine turning your harshest critic into your strongest ally. An agitated soul is often its own worst enemy, caught in loops of judgement and shame.

But learning to extend yourself mercy is the first step toward breaking that cycle. A quiet rebellion against the habits that are keeping you feeling small.

Simplify Your World: The power of decluttering—physically and mentally—can't be overstated. Chaos thrives in clutter, while calm struggles to breathe beneath it.

Picture a desk drawer overflowing with forgotten junk, and compare it to a mind tangled in worries, regrets, and endless to-do lists.

Just as clearing out that drawer makes room, so too does simplifying your world in any measure. It clears the way for clarity and calm. A cathartic process of shedding the weight that silently drags you under.

The less noise, the more space for serenity. Start small: one thought, one habit, one drawer at a time. Gradually, life begins to feel lighter, more spacious, easier to navigate.

Practise Gratitude: Bob Burg and John D. Mann, in *The Go-Giver*, remind us that true success and fulfillment don't come from accumulation, they grow from creating value for others.

Gratitude is the heartbeat of that philosophy.

When we give thanks for the richness already present in our lives, our attention tilts from agitation to appreciation. Gratitude soothes and steadies us; it starves restlessness.

As James, the protagonist in my first fiction novel asked:

> *"Life isn't about how much we consume; it's about how much we contribute. Why is that such a hard concept for people to grasp?"*

That sentiment distils the essence of this insight. Just as contributing eclipses consumption, *giving* thanks far outweighs the act of *receiving* it.

Gratitude isn't a passive feeling; it's an active practice, a daily recalibration of perspective that anchors you to what's nourishing, even when life feels lean.

Connect With Nature: Mindfulness and nature go hand in hand, like coffee and Monday mornings.

Yet in our modern lives, we spend far too much time indoors, disconnected from the grounding force of the natural world. I've felt the quiet reset that comes from stepping outside first-hand.

Nature humbles us. It reminds us how small we are, yet how deeply connected we can be.

Take a walk in the park. Sit by a river. Hike in the mountains if they're within reach. Nature's rhythms are everywhere, offering a silent invitation to slow down, observe, and recalibrate.

Even the simple act of watching leaves sway in the wind or listening to birdlife murmur overhead can soothe the most agitated soul.

Have you ever sat still long enough to hear pigeons in full concert? Their low, rhythmic coos create a soundtrack as calming as distant surf once you truly tune in.

The key is to look, listen, and let nature guide your mindfulness. There's no need for grand gestures, just presence.

Express Yourself: Madonna's been telling us for decades; *express yourself!* Creativity is cathartic, wildly therapeutic and often more effective than any formal intervention.

You don't need a therapist to know art, music, or writing can work remedial magic. Writing this book has been my own remedy; truthfully, much of my pent-up agitation came from neglecting creative pursuits for far too long. Once I returned to the page, the fog began to lift.

Do you enjoy painting, writing, music, or losing yourself any other form of artistic expression? Then what are you waiting for?

Creativity is more than producing something; it's about releasing, processing, and untangling emotions that might otherwise stay knotted in your mind.

Creative pursuits naturally foster mindfulness. They pull you into the present moment, where flow replaces friction and expression becomes a steadying and freeing meditation.

Set Healthy Boundaries: Protect your sanctuary of inner peace by setting boundaries that honour your energy.

Say *no* to what drains you, and *yes* to what nourishes you. It's an act of self-care but even more so, of self-respect.

Imagine building a cozy nook, shielded from external pressures and internal turmoil. Boundaries are more like gates than walls: they open to what serves you and close to what unsettles you.

The more intentional you are about what you allow into your space—physically, mentally, emotionally—the more sustainable your inner peace becomes.

Boundaries aren't barriers to connections; they're invitations to authenticity.

Look After Your Physical Health: Your physical health is a cornerstone of inner peace. When your body feels off, your pursuit of calm often slips. And the longer it does, the harder it is to claw your way back.

Healing isn't about comfort, it's about courage.

So, check in with yourself. Are you eating well? Drinking too much grown-ups' cordial? Moving your body enough? Minor adjustments make a major difference.

The trick is consistency over perfection.

You've seen this theme time and time again throughout the book. Start small. Habitualise it. Take another bite. Habitualise again. Rinse and repeat.

Bit by bit, it stacks up until one day it's second nature: your body supporting your mind like a well-tuned duet.

Look After Your Mental Health: It might seem bleedingly obvious given the subject matter, but let's address it head-on nonetheless: lean on the right people.

Inner calm isn't built in isolation; it's held together by the people and connections you trust.

Protecting your mind starts with choosing them wisely.

Turn to those who offer genuine empathy and understanding. Tread softly, however, because not everyone is wired that way.

Just because someone is family or close friend doesn't mean they can give you the support you need.

Opening up takes courage, but you've already proven you're a Phoenix on the rise. This is simply the next step in the journey.

If direct, personal support feels too close right now, consider broader networks. Support groups, online communities, or local initiatives can connect you without the pressure of deep personal ties.

In my neck of the woods, *Men's Shed* offers a place for men to gather, work on meaningful projects, and share skills in a friendly, supportive environment.

Perhaps there's something similar near you.

The key is participation. Invest energy in finding the right fit. Have conversations. Explore options.

A strong support system can make all the difference, not only in moments of crisis, but in the quiet, ongoing work of cultivating inner peace.

Live in the Present: Yes, we've touched on this too, but it bears repeating.

Living in the moment, unshackled from past regrets or future anxieties, neither of which you can influence, is a practice you must return to again and again. It cannot be overstated.

Embrace the present. When you find yourself drifting into rumination, acknowledge it, let it pass, and return to your mindfulness exercises.

Stick to your routines as best you can. Even a few minutes of conscious breath can immediately anchor you in the now.

The Power of Now, by German-born author Eckhart Tolle, illustrates this beautifully.

Drawing on personal experience, Tolle recounts his spiritual awakening; a transformation born from a period of deep depression and existential crisis in his late twenties.

According to legend, during one of his darkest nights he asked himself: *"If I'm not me, then who am I?"* That single reflection sparked an inner shift towards lasting peace.

His transformation came in recognising *the self* apart from *the ego*, just as yours began the moment your authentic self found its voice. Faint though it may be right now, that voice marks the beginning of your journey. Rest assured, it's on the rise.

The present moment isn't a refuge, it's where life actually happens. So sit on a quiet grassy knoll overlooking the beach, feel the breeze brush your skin, and chew on that for a bit.

Only Two Things in Life are True ...

We've explored resilience, self-compassion, and the power of presence. Now, let's close with one of life's few undeniable truths.

Eventually, peace finds us all. That much is certain. But shouldn't we fight for it while we're on this planet, instead of chasing what others call valuable? Don't just rest in peace, *live in it.*

Peace isn't something to wait for. It's something to cultivate, moment by moment, breath by breath.

And the sooner the better. A more meaningful life awaits.

As Mae West reminded us:

> *"You only live once, but if you do it right, once is enough."*

So don't wait for peace to knock quietly on your door. Invite it in. Make space for it. Feed it. Let it grow. And start to see your agitated soul not as your enemy, but as your teacher.

If you listen closely, you'll hear it whisper: *it's time to live in peace.*

The Calm Amidst the Chaos

15

The Agitation Autopsy

Let's be honest; most of us are juggling more than we care to admit.

In my own circles of family and friends, I can count the truly peaceful souls on one hand, and those teetering near equilibrium, perched mid-seesaw, on the other. Then there's the rest, piled high on the far end, weighed down by noise, speed, and quiet despair.

That ratio isn't flattering. The number of content, worry-free individuals is dwarfed by those silently fraying at the edges. I'm speaking only from experience within my modest networks, shaped by distant observations, and it's quite feasible I'm completely wrong. I *hope* I'm completely wrong.

But when I look out into city streets and shopping centres, I'm met with a sea of lifeless stares. Suppressed bitterness. Vacant eyes. And the conclusion I keep drawing; the one I find increasingly difficult to shake, is that this imbalance isn't just common. It's epidemic.

So let's not circle your agitated soul any longer. Let's zoom in. Let's watch it in action.

This chapter's a little different.

It's all about practice. You'll find a series of vignettes ahead; each laced with a little agitation and a touch of humour. They're sticky, real-life moments designed to stir something in you. Not to provoke, but to invite you to sit with each experience.

Here's what I'm suggesting. Read them twice in two complete passes.

First pass: bring calm intention. Imagine these moments are happening to you in real time. Try to apply the practices we've covered so far. If you need a refresher, flip to *The Calm Companion's Field Guide*. It's there to help you choose which tools to bring into play.

Second pass: observe your reactions. Notice what shifts in your body. What thoughts flare. What stories arise. This is your agitation autopsy. A chance to witness the cogs turning beneath the surface.

And one more thing. Play the self-compassion card. Step back. Imagine you're the trusted confidant, bringing empathy to the fight for your closest friend. That's the lens I want you to use.

I'll do my best to keep it light-hearted. But let's not pretend these situations aren't mentally taxing. I promise I'll go easy … mostly.

Thanks a Lot *Genius*!

More than once, I've come *this* close to starring in my own viral road rage YouTube video.

Thankfully, it's never made it to the first upload, but I know that *fuse-box-about-to-blow feeling all too well*. It's like there's a switch inside me labelled *'Do Not Touch'*, and yet, life just can't resist flicking it. You know what I'm talking about.

Let me set the scene.

You're stuck in traffic, late for a meeting, still stewing over the yelling match you had with your spouse before you left home.

You're hungry, you haven't had your morning coffee, and somewhere in the back of your mind, you're wondering if you can keep grinding away at this dead-end job when all you really want is time to write your poetry.

The sun's glaring off the bonnet, heat pooling in the cabin. The air feels thick enough to take a bite out of.

Finally, the traffic starts moving. Your turn's coming up, you time your move perfectly, so you won't hold anyone up, and the car beside you floors it, and blocks your run.

You see red. And just like that, you're officially pissed.

First read: Loosen your grip on the wheel (metaphorically). Breathe. Imagine letting this one slide without it owning your mood.

Second read: Notice your pulse, your jaw, your breath. What story did your mind start telling? Could you choose a different one?

The Staplers are in the Damn Stationery Cabinet *Genius…*

We've all been here, somewhere between simmering and full boil. The details may differ, but I'm betting you can map this to your own personal version.

You arrived at work late because some *genius* cut you off, forcing you to miss your turnoff.

You throw your bag under the desk and wrestle your glasses out of the front pocket in one rushed movement. It reminds you how much you hate wearing the damn things … and getting old.

You recalibrate forcing today's critical 4:00pm deadline to the front of your mind.

The Calm Amidst the Chaos

You set everything in place, ready to tackle the gargantuan task when suddenly, your attention is hijacked by an email notification flashing in the corner of your screen.

Out of *'obligation'* (aka habit), you open your inbox. Of the 188 unread overnight emails, your *conscious* mind latches onto:

Where's My Refund?
ICT Outage This Morning - Sorry for The Inconvenience
URGENT - *Please Respond Regarding Friday Drinks*
Nine More Items for the Project Scope – **Deadline: 4:00pm Today**
After 15 Years of Your Loyalty, I'm Taking My Account Elsewhere

You sigh, shove the chaos aside, and try to refocus. You're hungry and tired, and now you've run out of time to get your morning coffee.

Just then, your colleague pops his head over the partition and asks to borrow your stapler because he's run out of staples.

You see red. And just like that, you're officially pissed.

First read: Zoom your focus down to the one thing that matters right now. Let the inbox noise and stapler fiasco fade.

Second read: Track the chain reaction from the first email subject line to the stapler request. Where did the first domino fall, and how could you stop the next from toppling?

Can't You See I'm Already Overloaded *Genius*...

Apparently, you *"have a way with words."* So when the original speaker pulled out last minute, the CFO *volunteered* you to deliver a presentation at this morning's company-wide meeting.

The presentation is about the recently rolled out sales and accounting software. A package you know less than nothing about.

The CEO, CIO, CFO, GM, AGM ... and the janitor will be attending.

You were late for work because some *genius* cut you off costing you your turnoff. You're rattled, still haven't had your morning coffee, and you're mentally juggling the 4:00pm deadline while silently cursing the universe's questionable sense of humour.

You scramble for anything resembling intel on the sales and accounting package, as you try to forget that your *gift for gab* tends to falter when the topic makes you feel like a fraud.

After frantically cobbling together a lacklustre PowerPoint, you scribble a few speaking points on the back of your hand and head to the meeting.

To your surprise, you're first up after management's opening remarks.

Your palms are sweaty, your mouth is dry, and the chewing gum you're working over is dissolving from the acid leeching off your tongue.

You're summoned to the lectern. After a few awkward attempts, the presentation finally loads. You face the audience, and there, front and centre, sits the CFO staring through you with the dead-eyed disinterest of someone who'd rather be literally anywhere else.

You stumble through your opening, wrestling valiantly to marry content with delivery. Despite the chaos, you start to feel like you're actually getting on top of it ... until you glance at the CFO, who is yawning his ears off while *doomscrolling*, completely checked out.

You see red. And just like that, you're officially pissed.

First read: Plant yourself like a pro on stage. Deliver to the room, not the yawns. Let their faces blur into wallpaper while you keep your rhythm.

Second read: Replay the mental footage. When did the nerves flip into irritation? Was it the yawn, the scrolling, or something earlier? What else could you do to hold the line next time?

I Don't Have a Pot to Piss in *Genius*...

Despite being way behind on the deadline thanks to your botched presentation to the entire company this morning, hunger gets the better of you. You really need to eat.

You reach for your bag and dig around for your lunch, which seems to have vanished. You huff, wrestle your overloaded bag onto your lap, and tear at every zip like a surgeon desperate to save a failing operation.

You find everything you've ever lost—except your lunch. Pure betrayal. You must have left it on the kitchen bench at home.

You open your wallet. It's void of folding stuff, just a handful of coins. You grab your phone and dive into your banking app.

After three false attempts, your password is finally accepted. You look straight to your account balance, and there's barely enough to buy a stamp.

That triggers a mental avalanche: your home, car, and life insurances are all due next month. Gas, electricity, water, and rates the month after. And on top of it all, the family grocery bill has jumped 30% in the last quarter.

Suddenly, your thoughts turn to your kids and how ungrateful they are. They're not taking school seriously yet you're breaking your hump to put them through private school.

Your thoughts return to your growling intestinal tract.

You push back on your chair and stride toward the vending machine for a protein bar and a bag of chips, all the while wondering if you might need that money for petrol to get home. You inhale the protein bar like it owes you money on your way back to your desk to tackle that deadline.

As you arrive, your colleague is standing there with an envelope and a pen, asking for a $25 contribution towards a retirement gift for the CFO. Next week is his last before he cashes in his multi-million-dollar superannuation.

You see red. And just like that, you're officially pissed.

First read:
Let your shoulders drop. Imagine the missing lunch, the empty wallet, and the vending-machine guilt drifting past like clouds; nothing to grab, nothing to keep.

Second read:
Feel the weight in your gut. Is it hunger, frustration, or both? Track where it travels next: your jaw, your breath, your thoughts. At what point did the day's irritations start feeling overpowering?

Rock 'N' Roll *is* Noise Pollution *Genius*...

You leave work after what just might be the worst day of your life. You jump in your car, and your ruminating mind is in hyperdrive, chewing on the day from Hell.

Your car's AC died during the week, so you scrap with your tie, and roll all four windows down for relief from the torching sun before heading off.

Your spiralling thoughts circle back to the lunch debacle, and you begin stressing about how you're going to be able to afford to get the car's AC fixed.

You're instantly reminded of your dire financial situation. You glance hurriedly at the petrol gauge—you're running on fumes.

Your mind has shifted from runaway freight train to stealth bomber with a malfunctioning GPS and no flight plan.

Because you're so heavily distracted, you take a wrong turn and get railroaded down through the new extension to the motorway—a ten-lane behemoth that's going to make life a joy ... *one day.*

The Calm Amidst the Chaos

The noise from the construction site is deafening. Cranes clank, trucks thunder, steel screeches, and voices bark instructions that pierce your eardrums like hot needles.

You can't wind the windows up or you'll bake, so you crank up the radio as your only defence against the auditory onslaught.

The maverick stealth bomber in your head is now locked in a full-scale battle with your radio, and the carnage outside, each trying to out-scream the other.

The traffic is glacially slow, adding to your agitated state. You look ahead to see you're officially in gridlock. You're going to be stuck in that same spot for an age.

As you come to a complete stop, a fully loaded V8 monster crawls up beside you, AC/DC blasting on full volume. The windows are down, and the driver is *rockin' out* behind the wheel.

She turns to you, smiles peacefully, and gives you the *'rock 'n' roll fingers'*.

You see red. And just like that, you're officially pissed.

First read: Tune in to the soundscape: the clank of cranes, the roar of engines, the scream of guitars. Imagine letting each noise pass through you without sticking.

Second read: Notice which sound tightened your chest or clenched your jaw first. Was it the chaos outside, the music next to you, or the noise in your own head? How might you turn the volume down on just one of them?

I Didn't Do it on Purpose *Genius*...

You finally arrive home completely defeated. You drag your sorry arse to the front door.

Your damn keys are buried in the front compartment of your bag, and they simply refuse to be located. After 5 complete rounds of the compartment, an involuntary growl breaks out.

You dump everything at your feet and claw at every damn zipper like a paramedic trying to revive a flatline. You tear the bag wide open, and your belongings begin their escape.

Finally, you locate the damn keys, wrestle them free, unlock the door, then shove them, along with the other escapees back into the bag before they can stage an all-out rebellion.

You walk into the kitchen. Your spouse is already home. The familiar sights and sounds catapult this morning's yelling match back to the surface. You grunt an inaudible greeting.

> Agitation doesn't announce itself. It creeps in quietly, blending the trivial with the turbulent.

Before you even reach for the fridge door, your spouse, without so much as a glance in your direction, delivers their opening salvo:

"Why didn't you take your lunch to work? This is exactly what I was talking about this morning! You have no idea how much effort it takes for me to prep lunches before I leave for work … let's have it out, then!".

You open your mouth to retaliate, but nothing comes out. You're too tired to fight, too wired to let it go.

You see red. And just like that, you're officially pissed.

First read: Feel the shift as you cross the threshold from outside to inside. Imagine leaving the day's baggage, literal and emotional, at the door.

Second read: Notice the first spark: was it the memory of the morning, the tone of voice, or the words themselves? How might you step sideways instead of straight into the fire?

Stop Pointing Fingers *Genius*...

By day's end, you're exhausted, frustrated, and convinced the universe itself has conspired against you.

But has it? Or is something else at play here? Has your mind, trapped in the loop of agitation, started connecting dots that were never meant to be connected?

Throughout that hellish day, frustration built from the accumulation of unchecked agitation. Each moment fed the next, and it kept on snowballing with no respite in sight.

I know the scenarios were extreme; all crammed into a single brutal day. And let's be real, no one gets hit with *every* frustration like that, all at once.

But if you've lived in agitation long enough, you've felt this cycle. Only in real life, it's stretched out over weeks, months, or even years.

The irritants may vary, but the pattern stays the same. And that's where the problems compound.

Eventually, everything becomes someone else's fault, at least, that's how it's played out for me.

Hunger becomes the fault of others. The *genius* who cut you off in traffic somehow caused the fight with your spouse.

The CFO is now the reason you're not sipping tea in the sun and writing poetry.

And apparently, the loud, obnoxious V8 driver is responsible for your kids not taking school seriously.

That's the paradox of emotional bias—it manufactures a narrative that feeds its own self-interest and survival.

Is that cycle of blame a reasonable state of mind? Of course not. But in the heat of agitation, it *feels reasonable*. Because eventually, we run out of defence mechanisms, and the blame has to go somewhere.

We don't point fingers because we're cruel, we do it because we're tired, overwhelmed, and desperate to make sense of the madness.

And that's the problem.

The Hardest Thing to do is the Easiest Thing to Start

Here's the uncomfortable truth: you cultivated your agitation. Not intentionally, mind you. Not maliciously. But *through habit*.

Every time you reacted without mindfulness, every time frustration dictated your response, you reinforced it. You trained yourself over the years to be agitated first and mindful *never*.

Now imagine that same day without the seed of agitation.

A driver cuts you off, and you probably shrug it off and keep driving. The CFO yawns during your presentation? Whatever. His tired eyes aren't your problem.

Your kids not taking school seriously. Well, that turns into a conversation, not a resentment.

And the '*rock 'n' roll fingers*' is just a dudette vibing in her world.

The point is, none of these things can ruin your day unless you let them. Unless you *choose* to let them. So choose *not* to let them. Don't give them air. Flip the switch.

Why do we agitated souls find that so hard? Because hard-wired behaviours aren't like batteries you can swap out.

They're hardwired, and notoriously difficult to weed out, and that's precisely the point.

The Calm Amidst the Chaos

The hardest thing to do is the easiest thing to start once you know how to break the cycle. Stopping agitation *is* simple; deceptively so. Just choose not to react and let it go.

But when agitation is *all* you've ever known, that *choice* feels impossible, like waking up tomorrow fluent in Nepali.

That's why mindfulness is more than a concept; it's a process. It rewires how you engage with frustration, replacing reaction with awareness. And like any skill, it gets easier each time you practise.

You can unlearn agitation. Mindfulness and meditation can pave the way. If only we could swap out our agitated soul with a shiny new, transcendent one. Wouldn't that be lovely?

But we can't. We have to undo the past by making better choices in the present. Wisdom teaches us that.

The first time you attempt not to react with agitation will be brutal. Every fibre of your being will fight back, insisting frustration is the *only way*. But if you override it, just once, something shifts.

The hardest thing to do is often the easiest thing to start.

And each time after that it gets easier. Eventually, you won't have to think about it at all.

You'll be halfway to transcendence before you even realise you've begun.

Flip the Switch ... Really

Now that you've seen how agitation can hijack your body and mind, it's time to get tactical.

In the first pass through each vignette, you learned to spot the sensory trigger and clock its effect on you. In the second, you went deeper, observing your physiology, naming what's happening, and reframing your reaction in the moment.

This on-the-spot toolkit is the third layer. Once you've sharpened the first two, you can deploy these emotional tactics in real time, cutting off the hijack before it takes the wheel.

Together, the three stages form a potent process; one you can use against any mix-and-match combination of factors that would otherwise stir up your agitation.

Bring Calm to the Battle: Take a slow, deliberate breath and remember, the fight isn't with *them*, it's with the agitation trying to run the show. Tell yourself, *"That genius who cut me off is not the architect of my agitated soul."* You don't know their story, and you might have misread the moment entirely.

Bring Empathy to the Fight: Pause long enough to imagine the battle *they* might be fighting. One you can't see. Keep scanning for reasons to give them the benefit of the doubt.

Look for the flicker of humanity in their struggle and choose understanding over the muttered accusations your agitation is itching to deliver.

Bring Mindfulness to the Conflict: Let your eyes land on something solid and real: the texture of your desk, the weight of the steering wheel, the feel of your feet on the floor.

Breathe into that moment. This is you stepping out of the autopilot loop that's been fuelling your agitation and back into the driver's seat of your own mind.

Bring Meditation to the Frontline: Let the mindfulness you've just called in open the door a little wider. Step through it.

Give peace the prime position where agitation used to stand guard. Start small—a single slow breath, a minute of stillness—and let those moments stack over time.

Where reaction once barked orders, let stillness rule the roost.

Bring Physiological Awareness to the Storm: Pause and scan yourself like you're checking the rigging before the gale.

Where is the tension anchored? Feel where it lingers, where it grips, where it refuses to let go. Then loosen it. Unclench your jaw, drop your shoulders, soften your hands.

Exhale that weight you've been carrying without realising it.

Bring Positive Reframing to the Fray: Catch the story your agitation is trying to tell and rewrite it on the spot. Turn frustration into fuel by shaping the moment into something that works for you, not against you.

Instead of an annoyance, see it as a live-fire drill for patience and self-control — a chance to strengthen your footing before life throws its next punch.

Bring Gratitude to the Confrontation: In the heat of the moment, plant your feet in gratitude. Call to mind one thing, big or small, you're genuinely thankful for.

Let it fill the space your agitation was trying to occupy. Gratitude reshapes the battlefield, shifting your focus from what's wrong to what's right, and steadying your mind before the next blow can land.

Bring Distraction to the Clash: Blindside your agitation with something it didn't see coming. Break the loop by yanking your focus somewhere unexpected: blast your favourite song, count backwards from 100, recite the alphabet in reverse, or tackle a quick mental puzzle.

The aim is to throw your mind just far enough off balance that the cycle snaps, your mood rewires, and calm slips back into the driver's seat.

Bring Acceptance to the Encounter: Lay down your arms and step back from the skirmish. Some battles just aren't worth the energy.

Accept what's out of your control: the cut-off in traffic, the forgotten lunch, and let them shrink to their true size: minor blips in the grand sweep of your day. The moment you stop feeding them, the hijack loses its grip.

Bring Humour to the Party: Sometimes the fastest way to defuse frustration is to laugh straight in its face. Humour is your secret weapon. It slips past the guards your agitation posts at the door.

Turn the moment into comedy and watch its bite disappear. Picture the absurdity: your terrible day as a sitcom pilot, the V8 driver as your long-lost sibling, vibing unapologetically on their bad decisions.

Before You Holster the Toolkit

These aren't just coping tricks; they're part of your emotional arsenal. Use them often. Sharpen them daily. And when agitation comes knocking, you'll answer with calm, clarity … and maybe even a laugh.

But before you charge off into the sunset, a few ground rules if I may. I'd hate for any of these tactics to be misread or misused.

One of the fundamental principles in peacefully dealing with difficult situations is to practise acceptance.

Acceptance does not mean resigning yourself to a life of suffering or passively enduring hardship. Rather, it involves acknowledging the reality of the situation without judgement or resistance.

By accepting the present moment as it is, we free ourselves from the burden of futilely wishing for things to be different.

More to the point, it quiets the inner courtroom that's endlessly drafting arguments to prove your agitation is justified.

This acceptance allows us to focus our energy on finding constructive solutions. As we have discussed ad nauseum, mindfulness involves being *fully present in the moment*, without being consumed by regrets of the past or anxieties of the future.

Self-care plays a crucial role in maintaining inner peace during difficult times. Taking care of our physical, emotional, and mental well-being is essential for building resilience and coping with adversity.

Prioritising self-care is not a selfish act. It's an act of preservation. A necessary step towards building the strength and resilience needed to navigate life's challenges with grace and equanimity.

Self-compassion involves treating yourself with the same kindness and understanding that you would extend to a friend in need, especially when you feel least deserving of it.

Offering compassion to others, even in the midst of conflict or disagreement, can help bridge divides, foster understanding, and promote healing in challenging situations.

Why should self-compassion be any different? If anything, it's the foundation that makes compassion for others sustainable.

Healthy boundaries really do matter in the face of difficult circumstances. Setting clear boundaries with oneself and others can help prevent overwhelm, burnout, and resentment.

Learning to say no when necessary, prioritising your own needs, and communicating assertively yet respectfully can help promote balance and harmony in relationships and life situations.

I Think I'll Sleep Well Tonight...

And here's the cherry on top: life isn't getting easier: you're getting wiser.

Peacefully navigating life's difficult moments means putting mindfulness in the lead and then taking action.

Once you build a pattern of mindful response, it becomes muscle memory. Each time you choose calm over chaos, you strengthen the neural pathways of peace.

Unification is everything here: mind, body, breath, choice.

We've only scratched the surface. The examples may have been light-hearted, but they're universal.

Now it's your turn. Dig a little deeper into your own life. Find the friction points, and apply mindfulness not as theory, but as practice.

When mindfulness leads, meditation follows, adding another layer of protection against your agitated default.

It loses its grip. You stop reacting and start responding.

Seriously! Agitation doesn't deserve to be your baseline. Life is too short to keep feeding habits you inherited but never chose, and too precious to keep rehearsing reactions that never served you.

You've seen a better way. Now go live it.

The Calm Amidst the Chaos

16

Your Journey Forward

Now is a time of reflection; to pause and consider where you are, how you got here, and where you're heading next.

Honour the journey that brought you to this point. Every experience, joyful or painful, has shaped you in ways both subtle and profound.

Reflect on each setback. What did it teach you? Did it thicken your skin, or harden your heart?

Whatever the impact, resilience has been quietly building in you, layer by layer, moment by moment.

And every victory to come, no matter how small, will quietly reinforce the confidence that carries you forward, step after steady step.

This isn't just about looking back; it's about envisioning what's next. Be specific about your transformation. Be bold about what you aspire to. Imagine the day you are truly free from your agitated soul. What does *that* feel like?

How does it feel to step into a self that radiates authenticity and purpose?

Trust that you can navigate this path. You've already taken the first courageous step toward self-discovery. Be proud; you're on your way.

A gentle warning: *as this period of reflection unfolds, be kind to yourself. Understand that growth is not linear; it's filled with twists, turns, and surprises. Embrace this time as an opportunity for renewal; a chance to honour who you've been and also to celebrate who you're becoming.*

Intent Without Action is Just Drift

Reflection is powerful, but without action it's only drift. To create meaningful change, transform good intentions into deliberate, thoughtful steps. Align your actions with your values. Take responsibility for your outcomes.

There will be moments when the journey feels impossibly tough. I know because I've been there. When that happens, pause. Breathe. Reflect on how far you've come. Revisit your foundational practices, then realign and refocus.

To create meaningful change, you must transform good intentions into deliberate, thoughtful action.

Embrace the struggle as part of your story. From mindfulness and meditation, each challenge builds resilience and fortitude, not more agitation, not more habitual reaction.

Your strength is forged in these moments. Push through. Keep your eyes on the prize.

Let Your Resilience Shine Bright

This is your journey forward, towards a future where peace and resilience reign. A time when your spirit transcends agitation and your authentic self steps into the spotlight.

Breathe with mindfulness. Move with intention. Act with grace. Let calm flow through your days like a quiet river. Meet challenges with gentle strength and an unwavering sense of purpose.

One day soon, you'll navigate life's storms with grounded ease. Your resilience will shine brightly, not just for you, but as a beacon for others.

What a life: a sanctuary of tranquillity, where your soul finds solace and your heart beats with the rhythm of unshakable calm.

And as your resilience begins to shine, a choice awaits—one that will set the tempo for the next chapter of your life.

And when you turn the page, we'll stand together at a fork in the road, weighing the two paths, but only you can choose which one to take.

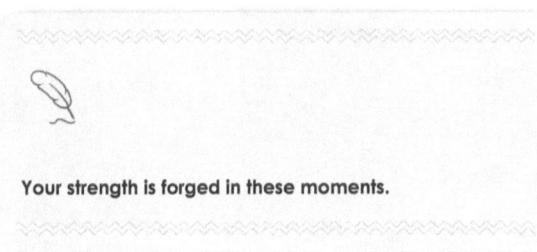

Your strength is forged in these moments.

The Calm Amidst the Chaos ✐

17

Embracing Your Transcendent Soul

Well, look at you; still here, still reading, still cogitating. You know what that tells me? It tells me you're invested, committed, already knee-deep in this transformation, whether you realise it or not.

So, now the real question is: what happens next?

The way I see it, you've arrived at that fork in the road. A place where you're faced with a choice that will shape the future you.

The road to the left leads towards the vision of the true, authentic self: the one you know you're destined to become.

The road to the right loops back to your old patterns and your *"sins of the past"*. The same weary roundabout you've circled before, and you know exactly where that leads, straight back into the arms of agitation.

The Calm Amidst the Chaos

Thankfully, two carriages are waiting at this fork to expedite your journey—let's call them *'Action'* and *'Intention'*. The most important decision you have to make now is which one you'll board.

Action will take you down the path to the left: it's express, uncertain, with peaks and valleys, but always moving forward.

Intention, on the other hand, is already coupled to the tracks that lead to the right, and it's *'stopping all stations'*, looping you back to where you began.

Action moves us forward; always forward. It's not without its challenges, but it's the only carriage that delivers change.

Intention feels like a choice for change, but in reality, it's just another ride around the loop. It's passive, deceptively comfortable, and dangerously easy to board.

The mistake isn't boarding the wrong carriage; it's stepping into *Intention*, thinking you've chosen *change*, when all you've really done is buy a first-class ticket back to exactly where you started.

From here on in, every stride forward will summon the triggers that feed your agitated soul. **They're inevitable, unavoidable — and your agitated soul will want to feast on every single one.** This is your moment to choose change and refuse to accept the old defaults. Your agitated soul will stir, but your transcendent self is ready to rise.

This reminds me of a humorous t-shirt I saw recently, which read:

'I said I'll fix it. If I said I'm gonna fix it, I'm gonna fix it. You don't have to bring it up every 6 months!'

That right there sums up the difference between action and intention, and why only one will ever change your life.

The Proof is in the Pudding

Now it's confession time. The words in this book resonate deeply with me.

I believe in them, and I stand by them, but here's the truth: my journey toward becoming a transcendent soul has only just begun.

Yep, I am still an agitated soul, an epiphany I was confronted with after finishing Chapter 15. I relived the bitter and distasteful emotions I used to drown in, as if that hellish day was unfolding in real time.

The Agitation Autopsy began as a bit of cheek—a playful way to drive home what I thought was a pretty solid point.

What I wasn't expecting was the physical reaction; the chest pains, the nausea, the shakes, every symptom reminding me exactly what it means to live as an agitated soul.

I couldn't shake it for hours.

But the washup also proved something else. It showed me just how far I've come. The belief in myself, the fortitude to keep striving for something better, a more authentic self.

And that makes me living proof that this path works. Despite only just beginning, I can feel the profound shift in my soul.

If I can feel this shift—this tremor of transformation—then so can you.

It's not miraculous, it's just momentum. Each small step forward makes the next one easier to take.

Now my life barely resembles the constant agitation I used to cling to with unsettling regularity. I thank the universe for these small blessings, and I cherish the chance to change.

The experience also reminded me, just like a recovering addict, it's easy to slip backward if you're not vigilant.

Most importantly, it reminded me of the Herculean task you are now facing, and that fills me with empathy for you, and a deep, unwavering pride in what you're about to achieve.

Well…What are you Waiting For?

Intentions don't change lives; actions do.

So, there's really not much left to say, only things to do.

You've walked this path to the fork in the road, reflected deeply, and faced yourself with honesty.

Now the real question is: are you ready? Not just in theory. Not just as a lofty esoteric idea. Are you truly ready to take your journey beyond these pages?

Are you ready to advance down the road to the left?

You know as well as I do, it's easy to hide behind *intention*. But intentions don't change lives: actions do. This is your defining moment, the point where thought must crossover into movement. Every step from here is proof you're not just dreaming about change, you're living it.

There is no more waiting for *'the right time'* or *'the perfect moment'*—*this is it.*

So, take another step. Just one. Not because I said so. Not because this book told you to. But because deep down, you already know … you are ready.

Trust yourself. Make the change.

Step forward with conviction, and when you eventually look back to assess your progress, you won't see an agitated soul; you'll see the moment you chose something greater.

Now go. The only thing standing between you and change is waiting ... and your transcendent soul won't wait.

The Calm Amidst the Chaos ✒

The Calm Companion
Field Guide

The Calm Amidst the Chaos

👀 Visual Index
A symbolic map of your Calm Companion's Field Guide

Icon	Section Title	Description
	Dear Reader,	A gentle welcome and invitation to return to calm
	Reader's Pledge	Your declaration of transformation and intention
	The Calm Covenant	A sacred agreement with your inner peace
	The Agitation Autopsy Roadmap	Practical Exercise layering to any real-life trigger.
	Affirmations	Anchoring truths to revisit and repeat
	Invictus	A poetic rally cry for resilience and defiance
	Mindfulness & Meditation Practices	Practical tools to cultivate presence and stillness
	Habit Transformation Tools	Strategies to rewire your patterns and reclaim agency
	Emotional Resilience Strategies	Ways to build strength, boundaries, and bounce-back
	Self-Compassion & Self-Care	Rituals to nourish your body, mind, and spirit
	Mindfulness in Battle	Tactical tools for staying grounded in chaos
	Foundational Insights	Core truths about habits, emotions, and transformation
	Starting the Journey	Encouragement to begin—gently, bravely, now
	Continuing the Journey	Questions to carry forward as you evolve
	Inner Mapping Tools	Archetypes and emotional decoding for self-awareness
	Emergency Calm Kit	A grab-and-go toolkit for moments of overwhelm
	The Mirror Questions	Reflective prompts to deepen your inner dialogue
	The Sting in the Tale (Reprise)	A closing truth to carry into the world

233

The Calm Amidst the Chaos

Dear Reader,

This companion is more than a summary, it's a refuge. A place to return to when the world gets loud, when your soul feels frayed, when you simply need to remember what you've already learned.

Use it gently. Use it boldly. Use it as often as you need.
You've earned your calm, so keep it close.

—Gerard

Reader's Pledge

A declaration of courage, compassion,

and conscious transformation.

I acknowledge my agitated soul not as a flaw, but as a teacher.
I commit to practising mindfulness and meditation:

- *in awareness*
- *with compassion*
- *with courage*
- *without judgement.*

I will honour my transformation—one breath, one choice,
one moment at a time.

Signed: _____
Date: _____

🕊 The Calm Covenant

A sacred agreement between you and your inner peace.
**What does calm mean to you today?
Write it down. Let it evolve.**

📖 Agitation Autopsy Roadmap

A universal process for applying the First Read / Second Read / Practical Exercise layering to any real-life trigger.

🎯 First Read

Pause. Breathe. Imaging letting the moment pass without it owning you.

🎯 Second Read

Notice your body, breath, and thoughts. Identify the exact moment the shift happened.

🎯 Practical Exercises

Apply the most relevant Calm Companion tool (e.g., reframing, grounding, humour, boundaries) to reset your state.

Use this sequence for traffic jams, office politics, family tension—any time your agitated soul stirs.

Over time, this roadmap becomes second nature. A quiet automatic pivot from reaction to response. Each pass through the sequence strengthens your awareness, sharpens your choices, and builds the muscle of calm.

The more you use it, the faster you'll recognise the early tremors of agitation and meet them with grounded clarity. In that moment, you're in command of the story that follows, not at the mercy of the trigger.

🪴 Inspirational Anchors

🔥 Identity & Ownership

"Only by knowing the source of my agitation can I be free of it."
"If you refuse to change, you choose to accept."
"You cultivated your agitation. Now you can unlearn it."
"Your agitated soul is not a flaw—it's a teacher."
"You are not broken. You are becoming."
"Are you truly living, or are you merely existing?"
"I think, therefore I am." – René Descartes

🧠 Mindfulness & Awareness

"Mindfulness is not a theory—it's a process."
"The hardest thing to do is the easiest thing to start."
"Present-moment awareness is the culmination of everything we've explored."
"Mindfulness is the art of noticing. Meditation is the art of surrender."
"Life is not playing out in your mind—it's playing out around you."
"Life's a journey, not a destination." – Steven Tyler

💪 Resilience & Courage

"Let your agitation be the fire that forges your greatness."
"Progress over perfection."
"Transformation is not comfortable—it comes from change that shakes you."
"You've already proven you're a Phoenix on the rise."
"Resilience isn't just collective—it's personal."
"You have nothing to fear but fear itself." – Franklin D. Roosevelt (often misattributed to MLK)

💗 Self-Compassion & Healing

"Self-compassion is healing, and it begins with how you speak to yourself."
"Your battle scars can become your armour."
"Be the compassionate king of your own kingdom."
"The discipline of writing something down is the first step to getting it done."
– Lee Iacocca

Purpose & Transcendence

"Let your transcendent soul rise, not in spite of agitation, but because of it."
"You've seen a better way. Now go live it."
"Your agitated soul isn't your enemy; it's an invitation to dance differently."
"Choose to be a Phoenix ... Rise."
"Twenty minutes of doing something meaningful is more valuable than twenty hours of thinking about doing it."
"He who has a why to live can bear almost any how." – Friedrich Nietzsche
"You only live once, but if you do it right, once is enough." – Mae West

---

Invictus

by William Ernest Henley
(A poem for the soul that refuses to bow)

Out of the night that covers me,
Black as the pit from pole to pole,
I thank whatever gods may be
For my unconquerable soul.

In the fell clutch of circumstance
I have not winced nor cried aloud.
Under the bludgeonings of chance
My head is bloody, but unbowed.

Beyond this place of wrath and tears
Looms but the Horror of the shade,
And yet the menace of the years
Finds and shall find me unafraid.

It matters not how strait the gate,
How charged with punishments the scroll,
I am the master of my fate,
I am the captain of my soul.

🧘 Mindfulness & Meditation Practices

- Create a quiet, distraction-free space
- Start with short sessions to build your meditation muscles
- Focus on your breath to stay present
- Accept wandering thoughts without judgement
- Experiment with different techniques
- Be consistent and patient
- Practise deep listening
- Observe your surroundings
- Engage in mindful eating
- Embrace mindful movement
- Practise gratitude

♻ Habit Transformation Tools

- Identify triggers and cues
- Replace negative habits with positive alternatives
- Practise mindfulness and self-awareness
- Set specific, achievable goals
- Use positive reinforcement
- Create a supportive environment
- Practise consistency and persistence
- Seek professional guidance
- Mindful breathing
- Body scan meditation
- Urge surfing

- The S.T.O.P. method
- Mindful journaling
- Loving-kindness meditation

🎗 Emotional Resilience Strategies

- Separate triviality from tribulation
- Listen to the universe
- Embrace the flow of change
- Find strength in vulnerability
- Transform obstacles into opportunities
- Practise mindfulness and compassion
- Set boundaries to protect your energy
- Seek solace in solitude
- Believe in your resilience

🌱 Self-Compassion & Self-Care Techniques

- Practise self-compassion
- Simplify your world
- Practise gratitude
- Express yourself creatively
- Set healthy boundaries
- Look after your physical health
- Look after your mental health
- Live in the present

⚔ Mindfulness in Battle

- Bring calm to the battle
- Bring empathy to the fight
- Bring mindfulness to the conflict
- Bring meditation to the frontline
- Bring physical awareness to the storm
- Bring positive reframing to the fray
- Bring gratitude to the confrontation
- Bring distraction to the clash
- Bring acceptance to the encounter
- Bring humour to the party

Bring your whole self. Let calm be your shield.

Foundational Insights

Understanding Habits

Habits are formed through neural pathways that link cues, routines, and rewards. By identifying triggers, practising mindfulness, and replacing negative habits, you can rewire your brain for lasting change.

Navigating Life's Challenges

Life's curveballs are inevitable, but your responses define you. Prioritise what truly matters. Embrace change, vulnerability, and transformation.

Embracing Self-Compassion

Forgive yourself. Celebrate small victories. Balance accountability with grace. Protect your energy and seek solitude when needed.

Acknowledging Your Agitated Soul

Recognition is the first step. Agitation shouldn't define you—it's part of your experience, and you have the power to change it.

The Power of Self-Reflection

Explore your formative years. Observe your emotions without judgement. Understanding is the gateway to peace.

Mindfulness & Meditation: Distinct but Complementary

Mindfulness anchors you in the now. Meditation offers retreat. Together, they build emotional stability and self-awareness.

🚪 Starting the Journey

It doesn't matter where you begin—just begin.
Start small.
Start gently.
Start now.
Every small victory builds momentum.
And momentum is how transformation begins.

⛩ Continuing the Journey

Before you close this book, ask yourself:

What tools will I carry forward?
What truths will I revisit?
What part of my agitated soul will I honour as I grow?
What boundaries will I protect to safeguard my peace?
Where will I choose action over intention in the days ahead?
How will I remind myself of my progress when the road feels long?
Who in my life will benefit most from the calm I now carry?

You've earned your calm—carry it with courage.

Inner Mapping Tools

 Navigational Archetypes

Archetype	Description
The Agitated Soul	Restless, reactive inner self, often misunderstood.
The Authentic Self	Calm, grounded, wise. Your destined nature.
The Ego Puppet	A protective mask worn to perform or defend.
The Inner Child	Vulnerable, curious, longing to be heard. Often neglected.
The Transcendent Soul	Integrated, empowered, and deeply aligned. Your *Authentic Self*.

 The Emotional Bias Decoder

Raw Emotion → False Belief → Habitual Reaction

- Mistakes = Humiliation → Don't try
- Ignored = I don't matter → Withdraw
- Criticism = Attack → Defend or lash out
- Failure = Final → Give up

Rewrite Prompt:

- **Mistakes = Momentum**
- **Ignored ≠ Invisible**
- **Criticism = Opportunity to grow**
- **Failure = Feedback**

🧰 Emergency Calm Kit

This is a grab-and-go list for when you are in the thick of the fight:

- 3 deep breaths
- Name the emotion
- Find one thing to be grateful for
- Use the S.T.O.P. method
- Picture your agitated soul in costume
- Say: "This is a moment of suffering. I choose compassion."
- Repeat your mantra
- Step outside (even for 60 seconds)
- Text someone who gets it
- Revisit your favourite page or passage

🌈 The Mirror Questions

- What does my agitated soul sound like when it speaks?
- What does my authentic self want me to know today?
- What am I clinging to that's no longer serving me?
- What would self-compassion look like in this moment?
- What am I afraid to feel, and why?
- What truth am I ready to live today?
- Where in my life am I mistaking comfort for peace?
- What would I do differently if I trusted myself completely?

The Sting in the Tale (Reprise)

"Maybe it's not about transcending our agitated soul but using it as a powerful force for even greater change."

The Calm Amidst the Chaos

Secret Chapter

The Sting in the Tale

Dear Agitated Soul,

Acknowledging my agitated soul was positively cathartic. That recognition gave me the power to confront it head-on. Why? Because I wanted to initiate change.

But there's a question that's been burning that still haunts me: why was I allowed to become an agitated soul in the first place? If one believes in a higher power, as I do, then one must question why this was permitted.

Could it be that we agitated souls are meant for something greater?

If you're anything like me, you question everything, challenge everything, and refuse to accept what doesn't sit right. The apathetic accept anything and challenge nothing—not me. I'm convinced I don't belong among the apathetic masses. And maybe the same could be said for you.

Perhaps we're on the cusp, teetering precariously between magnificence and mediocrity. And maybe, just maybe, agitation is the tension that keeps us from falling into the ordinary.

If that's the case, then where will our agitated souls lead us?

Maybe we were always destined to be agitated souls (because I for one certainly didn't volunteer for it), and there is a greater purpose afoot. Is there a divine presence? Who knows? But if there is, then perhaps agitation is less a punishment and more a proving ground for greater things.

Whatever the answer, I can tell you one thing straight up: given the choice between drifting in mediocrity or rising through agitation for greater purpose—I choose the latter, every time.

So, my parting words to you are these: I am incredibly proud of you for recognising the part of you that probably causes most of your pain. I applaud you for having the courage to address it.

Your agitated soul is a significant part of who you are; not because you chose it, but because it is. And although we agitated souls must change for the greater good, I believe there's a part of that agitated soul that sets us apart.

So as much as I want you to transcend your agitated soul, I also want to remind you: perhaps, just perhaps, there's a part of it worth holding on to.

Maybe it's less about transcending your agitated soul and more about transcending the apathy that surrounds you. Using what you've learned from your agitated existence for greater things.

Recognise that our inner turmoil is not a curse, but a catalyst. A spark for courage, growth, and change. While we may not have consciously chosen this path, it may have shaped us to transcend the ordinary and lead the way for others.

Let us carry the torch for our restlessness and harness it; not as something to defy, but as a powerful force to transcend the apathetic ordinary. Let it burn—not to destroy, but to illuminate.

Remember: maybe it's not about transcending our agitated souls, but using them as a powerful force for even greater change.

May the universe bring you all the courage you require.

And may your agitated soul *burn everlasting*,
but just bright enough to light the way for others.

THE END

www.ingramcontent.com/pod-product-compliance
Lightning Source LLC
Chambersburg PA
CBHW020523080526
44583CB00013B/718